American Culture in Peril

American Culture in Peril

Edited by
Charles W. Dunn

 UNIVERSITY PRESS OF KENTUCKY

Scholarly publisher for the Commonwealth,
serving Bellarmine University, Berea College, Centre College of Kentucky,
Eastern Kentucky University, The Filson Historical Society, Georgetown
College, Kentucky Historical Society, Kentucky State University, Morehead State
University, Murray State University, Northern Kentucky University, Transylvania
University, University of Kentucky, University of Louisville, and Western
Kentucky University.
All rights reserved.

Editorial and Sales Offices: The University Press of Kentucky
663 South Limestone Street, Lexington, Kentucky 40508-4008
www.kentuckypress.com

16 15 14 13 12   5 4 3 2 1

Library of Congress Cataloging-in-Publication Data

American culture in peril / edited by Charles W. Dunn.
    p. cm.
  Includes bibliographical references and index.
  ISBN 978-0-8131-3602-8 (hardcover : acid-free paper) —
  ISBN 978-0-8131-3603-5 (ebook)
  1. United States—Social conditions—21st century. 2. Politics and culture—
United States. 3. Social values—United States—History—21st century.
4. Social change—United States—History—21st century. 5. United States—
Civilization—21st century. 6. Cultural pluralism—United States—History—21st
century. 7. Liberalism—Social aspects—United States. 8. Conservatism—Social
aspects—United States. 9. Reagan, Ronald—Influence. I. Dunn, Charles W.
  E169.Z83A54 2012
  973.93—dc23   2012003414

This book is printed on acid-free paper meeting
the requirements of the American National Standard
for Permanence in Paper for Printed Library Materials.

Manufactured in the United States of America.

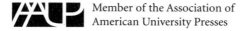 Member of the Association of
American University Presses

CONTENTS

Preface   vii

Introduction: The American Cultural Kaleidoscope   1
Charles W. Dunn

Part 1. Ronald Reagan and Modern Culture

Ronald Reagan and Modern Liberalism   13
Charles R. Kesler

A Touch for First Principles: Reagan and the Recovery of
Culture   33
Hadley Arkes

Part 2. Cultural Conflict in America

The Fickle Muse: The Unpredictability of Culture   55
Paul A. Cantor

Will the Postfamily Culture Claim America?   79
Allan Carlson

The Critic and Culture   97
Jean Bethke Elshtain

Part 3. The Possibilities of Cultural Change

Two Cities, How Many Cultures?   115
Ken Myers

Sources of Renewal in Twenty-first-Century America   135
Wilfred M. McClay

List of Contributors   155
Index   159

PREFACE

Seven years ago Regent University established the annual Symposium in Honor of Ronald Reagan, designed to bring to the campus leading scholars and public intellectuals to discuss matters of vital importance to American culture and society. The response of the public has been impressive:

- C-SPAN has aired the symposia;
- Several books from the symposia have garnered favorable critic reviews; and
- Audiences of 500 to 700 have attended each symposium.

The scholars and public intellectuals who have lectured include Jean Bethke Elshtain (Chicago), Brandice Canes-Wrone (Princeton), Harvey Mansfield (Harvard), George Edwards (Texas A&M), Jeffry Tulis (Texas), Hugh Heclo (George Mason), Hadley Arkes (Amherst), Daniel Dreisbach (American), George Nash (the Kirk Center), Stephen Knott (U.S. Naval War College), Michael Novak (American Enterprise Institute), Paul Cantor (Virginia), Charles Kesler (Claremont), Michael Barone (the *Washington Examiner*), Andrew Busch (Claremont), William Kristol (the *Weekly Standard*), James Ceaser (Virginia), Stephen Hayward (the American Enterprise Institute), Marvin Olasky (*World* magazine), Robert Spitzer (SUNY), Peter Lawler (Berry College), Wilfred McClay (Tennessee—Chattanooga), Ken Myers (Mars Hill Audio), Allan Carlson (Hillsdale), and Steven Skowronek (Yale). And critical reviews of the books emanating from the symposia include the following:

- The *New York Times* (October 7, 2007) review of *The Future of Conservatism: Conflict and Consensus in the Post-Reagan Era* (2007), by Jonathan Rauch (Brookings Institution), says, "[It] is as smart and stimulating a collection of political essays as

I've read in years, in part because it soars above the partisan potshots and petty maneuvering that preoccupy the political commentariat."

- Of *The Future of Religion in American Politics* (2009), Peter Augustine Lawler (Berry College) writes, "[It] is a genuinely outstanding collection of brilliant and accessible essays by many of the leading authorities on religion and politics in America. Many of the essays could easily stand alone as the best introduction to religion and politics available."

- Robert G. Kaufman (Pepperdine University) says of *The Enduring Reagan* (2009), "[It is] hands-down the finest compilation on Ronald Reagan," and "No compilation comes close to matching its insight and credibility."

- *The Presidency in the Twenty-first Century* (2011) earned the following blind, prepublication review by a critic: "The contributors constitute a veritable Who's Who of leading scholars on the American Presidency and their essays meet the high standard that one would expect from such illustrious authors. . . . The essays are not only timely, but in some ways timeless."

The stage is set, then, for *American Culture in Peril,* which treats a subject of keen interest not only to President Reagan, but also to a large cross section of American scholars and public intellectuals. Not everyone agrees with President Reagan's assessment of American culture, but who could disagree that his views set the stage for a lively debate about the matter? And who could disagree with the notion that culture is like the rudder on a ship, determining the nation's direction? As defined, the cultural rudder is "a guiding or controlling force or influence" in American society. In short, culture is at the heart of what America is and where it is going.

Ronald Reagan: Setting the Stage for Debate

Thirty years or so ago, when America struggled from the decade-long malaise of the 1970s, Ronald Reagan rejected the notion that the sun had set on a once-great country. He countered: "It's morning in America." Which reflected not only his optimism but also his belief that Americans must fight to retain the foundation for their optimism.

- "Freedom is a fragile thing and is never more than one generation away from extinction. It is not ours by inheritance; it must be fought for and defended constantly by each generation, for it comes only once to a people. Those who have known freedom, and then lost it, have never known it again."[1]
- "You and I have a rendezvous with destiny. We will preserve for our children this, the last best hope of man on earth, or we will sentence them to take the first step into a thousand years of darkness. If we fail, at least let our children and our children's children say of us we justified our brief moment here. We did all that could be done."[2]
- "America represents something universal in the human spirit. I received a letter not long ago from a man who said, 'You can go to Japan to live, but you cannot become Japanese. You can go to France and not become a Frenchman. You can go to live in Germany or Turkey, and you won't become a German or a Turk.' But then he added, 'Anybody from any corner of the world can come to America to live and become an American.'"[3]

What better time than now, when America once again faces potent challenges to its identity at home and abroad, to reexamine the character of American culture?

- Can a traditional view of American culture successfully compete against postmodernism?
- What are the sources of cultural renewal in a divided, pluralistic country?
- Is the promotion of traditional American cultural values merely an antiquated relic of Ronald Reagan's political movement?

Beginning especially with the housing crisis in 2007, political leaders have championed national governmental action as the primary solution to the nation's increasingly complex problems. Almost overnight, the country's perceived strength as a nation became intertwined with the level of governmental activity. This secular, government-centric view of America reflects a radical departure from Reagan's view of America's fundamental strength:

> I want you to know that this administration is motivated by a political philosophy that sees the greatness of America in you, her people, and in your families, churches, neighborhoods, communities—the institutions that foster and nourish values like concern for others and respect for the rule of law under God.
>
> Now, I don't have to tell you that this puts us in opposition to, or at least out of step with, a prevailing attitude of many who have turned to a modern-day secularism, discarding the tried and time-tested values upon which our very civilization is based. No matter how well intentioned, their value system is radically different from that of most Americans. And while they proclaim that they're freeing us from superstitions of the past, they've taken upon themselves the job of superintending us by government rule and regulation. Sometimes their voices are louder than ours, but they are not yet a majority.[4]

Ronald Reagan harnessed the power of the presidency to encourage Americans to return to their fundamental roots of faith, family, and freedom. More importantly, Reagan encouraged Americans to look beyond the grim headlines of daily newspapers and recognize the truth that still resided in their countrymen's hearts: "Now, I'm sure that you must get discouraged at times, but you've done better than you know. . . . There's a great spiritual awakening in America, a renewal of the traditional values that have been the bedrock of America's goodness and greatness."[5]

AMERICA'S CULTURAL RUDDER EXAMINED

Was Ronald Reagan right? Or did he engage in wishful thinking? The introduction to this volume casts doubt on the possibility of restoring a Reaganesque culture, because of increasing conflicts and tension, which impede the achievement of cohesion in American society. Reagan's aspirations for American culture would require greater cultural cohesion than is now on the horizon. But although that may be true, an in-depth examination of American culture always merits consideration, because culture is the rudder of American society.

In part 1, "Ronald Reagan and Modern Culture," Charles R. Kesler looks at the conflicts between "Ronald Reagan" and "Modern Liberalism," while Hadley Arkes considers the reclamation potential of a Reaganesque culture in "A Touch for First Principles: Reagan and the Recovery of Culture."

In part 2, "Cultural Conflict in America," Paul A. Cantor discusses "The Fickle Muse: The Unpredictability of Culture," Allan Carlson probes the question "Will the Postfamily Culture Claim America?" and Jean Bethke Elshtain focuses on "The Critic and Culture."

In part 3, "The Possibilities of Cultural Change," Ken Myers explores the ever-important relationship between the church and culture, and Wilfred M. McClay presents "Sources of Renewal in Twenty-first-Century America."

Nothing is more important to America's future than its culture. As sociologist Robert N. Bellah points out, values enable a society to maintain cohesion by producing "a basic cultural legitimation for a society, which is viewed as at least approximately in accord with them."[6] To what extent do today's American values provide "a basic cultural legitimation" for American society? That is the question at the heart of *American Culture in Peril*.

NOTES

1. Ronald Reagan, first inaugural address as governor of California, January 5, 1967.

2. Ronald Reagan, "A Time for Choosing," a speech on behalf of Senator Barry Goldwater's presidential campaign, 1964.

3. Ronald Reagan, a speech at a campaign rally for Vice President George H.W. Bush, San Diego, CA, November 7, 1988.

4. Ronald Reagan, remarks at the annual convention of the National Association of Evangelicals, Orlando, FL, March 8, 1983.

5. Ronald Reagan, *Speaking My Mind: Selected Speeches* (New York: Simon and Schuster, 2004), 175.

6. Robert N. Bellah, *The Broken Covenant: American Civil Religion in a Time of Trial* (New York: Seabury Press, 1975), ix.

Introduction

The American Cultural Kaleidoscope

Charles W. Dunn

> Any coherent and viable society rests on a common set of moral understandings about good and bad, right and wrong, in the realm of individual and social action. It is almost as widely held that *these common moral understandings must also rest in turn upon a common set of religious understandings* that provide a picture of the universe in terms of which the moral understandings make sense. Such moral and religious understandings produce both *a basic cultural legitimation for a society* which is viewed as at least approximately in accord with them, and *a standard of judgment* for the criticism of society that is seen as deviating too far from them. [Emphasis supplied]
> —Robert N. Bellah

Like the constantly changing patterns of light produced by a kaleidoscope, a broad and changeable array of values distinguishes American culture. Focusing on the values themselves, though—the product of the kaleidoscope—presents a daunting task, much like piecing together a mosaic of fragments without benefit of the artist's vision of the finished work. Since the constantly changing patterns of light are not a cause but a result, profit rests in an examination of the causes and consequences of the kaleidoscopic values in American culture.

First though, how important are values in a culture? Exceedingly important, because culture is like a constellation of all the ideas, habits, values, prejudices, and institutions that make up a society. In short, culture reflects the attitudes and behavior patterns of a society.

As sociologist Robert N. Bellah points out, values enable a society to maintain cohesion by producing "a basic cultural legitimation for a society which is viewed as at least approximately in accord with them, and a standard of judgment for the criticism of society that is seen as deviating too far from them." To what extent do today's American values provide "a basic cultural legitimation" and "a standard of judgment" for American society?

Moral and religious understandings in America have moved along a continuum from uniformity to diversity and from simplicity to complexity, and nowhere is that more evident than in surveying the changes in America's religious values. To illustrate, consider how far Harvard University has traveled from its origins. When founded, Harvard's charter expressed this purpose: "Everyone shall consider the main end of his life to know God and Jesus Christ which is eternal life."[1] No longer representative of the institution it governs, this charter demonstrates the conflict wrought by the kaleidoscopic nature of America's moral and religious understandings.

When Alexander Solzhenitsyn delivered his controversial commencement address at Harvard University in 1978, he highlighted the conflict between the historic Christian faith and the emerging faith of humanism: "The humanistic way of thinking . . . started Western civilization on the dangerous trend of worshipping man and his material needs."[2] Echoing Solzhenitsyn's analysis, although opposed to his position, John Dunphy states: "The classroom . . . will become an arena of conflict between the old and the new—the rotting corpse of Christianity . . . and the new faith of humanism."[3] Stark contrast and strident conflict now mark America's moral and religious understandings.

Ironically, the two sides in this and other conflicts about the moral and religious moorings of American culture share very similar understandings about fundamental values. They may place different emphases upon these values, but all the time they emphatically contend for their legitimacy. So whether the values are economic or political or religious or social, they constitute the underpinnings of American culture. The differing emphases upon them are what produces the kaleidoscopic result. Simultaneously, therefore, these values unify and divide.

THE FUNDAMENTAL VALUES OF AMERICAN CULTURE

What are these fundamental values of American culture? Even in their presentation, disagreement arises. In what order should they appear, and what emphasis should be placed on each? While we cannot resolve the disputes about either their order or their relative importance, at least we can briefly and comfortably set forth ten values, which emanate in the main from the wellspring of the Declaration of Independence and the Constitution, as the underpinnings of American culture.

1. Equality. The Declaration of Independence holds that "all men are created equal," a statement that refers to the equality of citizens before the law and in their rights to compete for jobs, income, status, and education on an equal footing with others.
2. Liberty. The Declaration of Independence also affirms that citizens have "certain unalienable rights, [and] that among these are the rights to life, liberty and the pursuit of happiness." Liberty as traditionally understood signifies that individuals have the freedom to seek their own best interests within limited restraints.
3. Property. Granting individuals the right to own property provides them with a primary means to find their place in society and to determine what they would like to do with their lives. Property ownership is a fundamental vehicle of self-expression and an important corollary of equality and liberty. So the Fourth and Fifth Amendments to the Constitution state:

> The right of the people to be secure in their persons, houses, papers, and effects, against unreasonable searches and seizures, shall not be violated, and no warrants shall issue, but upon probable cause, supported by oath or affirmation, and particularly describing the place to be searched, and the persons or things to be seized.
>
> No person shall be ... deprived of life, liberty, or property, without due process of law; nor shall private property be taken for public use without just compensation.

4. Opportunity. Sometimes called "rugged individualism," opportunity refers to rewarding personal effort and achievement rather than a person's social class, family standing, or some other arbitrary privilege that has not been personally earned. Again the opening of the Declaration of Independence underscores this value: "We hold these truths to be self-evident, that all men are created equal, that they are endowed by their Creator with certain unalienable rights, that among these are life, liberty and the pursuit of happiness." Individuals have the right to exercise their opportunities in the pursuit of happiness.

5. Democracy. Often called the "rule of law," democracy denotes that governmental power must be exercised within constitutional limitations as stipulated by the people, based upon two Greek root words for democracy, *demos* and *kratis,* meaning "people govern." Thus it was that America's Founders stated in the Declaration of Independence that to secure the rights of "life, liberty and the pursuit of happiness . . . governments are instituted among men, deriving their just powers from the consent of the governed."

6. Duty. The desirability of serving as a "good citizen" by participating in politics and community affairs, voting, and being tolerant of opposing views finds lodging in many places throughout the Declaration of Independence and the Constitution. For example, the Declaration of Independence begins as follows:

> When, in the course of human events, it becomes necessary for one people to dissolve the political bands which have connected them with another, and to assume among the powers of the earth, the separate and equal station to which the laws of nature and of nature's God entitle them, a decent respect to the opinions of mankind requires that they should declare the causes which impel them to the separation. . . .
>
> That whenever any form of government becomes destructive to these ends, it is the right of the people to

alter or to abolish it, and to institute new government, laying its foundation on such principles and organizing its powers in such form, as to them shall seem most likely to effect their safety and happiness.

The Constitution's First Amendment protects various means of expression, such as religion, speech, press, and assembly, which enable citizens to perform their duties as "good citizens."

7. Efficacy. The duty of serving as a good citizen would mean little if the citizenry did not believe their participation in public life could make a difference. At the heart of the Declaration of Independence and the Constitution is belief in the efficacy of the citizenry. Popular participation makes a difference. The fact that for more than two hundred years, a new government has operated under the Constitution, along with the many changes made to the Constitution, illustrates the value of popular efficacy in American culture. The civil rights movement is one of the best-known examples.

8. Community. American culture rests upon not just the rights of individuals, but also their rights to participate in community. This value emphasizes substantial deference to the role of the community in defining society's standards and providing stability from generation to generation. Community connects individuals in common causes. Nowhere was this more forcefully displayed than in the last line of the Declaration of Independence: "And for the support of this declaration, with a firm reliance on the protection of Divine Providence, we mutually pledge to each other our lives, our fortunes and our sacred honor." Neighborhood organizations, local schools, churches, service organizations, and other groups illustrate the value Americans place on community.

9. Religion. The Declaration of Independence begins thusly: "When, in the course of human events, it becomes necessary for one people to dissolve the political bands which have connected them with another, and to assume among the powers of the earth, the separate and equal station to which *the laws*

of nature and of nature's God entitle them, a decent respect to the opinions of mankind requires that they should declare the causes which impel them to the separation" (emphasis supplied). In part the Founders premised their very right to dissolve their ties to England on their theological understandings. And in the First Amendment to the Constitution, the first right granted was this: "*Congress shall make no law respecting an establishment of religion, or prohibiting the free exercise thereof*; or abridging the freedom of speech, or of the press; or the right of the people peaceably to assemble, and to petition the Government for a redress of grievances" (emphasis supplied).

10. Meritocracy. America's Founders rejected the European idea of a titled aristocratic ruling class based upon family and class standing. They adopted instead the idea of a "natural aristocracy," which anyone could join by virtue of merit and ability. This "natural aristocracy" includes, among others, those officials elected in a republican democracy to represent the people and to protect against the tyranny of the majority. Republican government or a representative democracy balances power between direct popular rule and centralized authoritarian rule. In the three branches of government spelled out in the Constitution, opportunities emerge for the development of a "natural aristocracy," which balances power between minority rights and majority rule.

Because these ten values exist in a highly pluralistic society, two questions emerge: How has pluralism influenced America's cultural kaleidoscope? And to what extent, if at all, should moral and religious understandings influence public life and democratic decision making in America? Two conflicting answers, with many variations in between, illustrate the complexity these questions pose. Always at least somewhat heterogeneous, America has accommodated and adjusted to the competing interests of a variety of ethnic groups, races, classes, and religious faiths. But does pluralism, which allows these competing interests to coexist, leave society devoid of moral and religious understandings and a sense of direction?

CONSEQUENCES OF TODAY'S CULTURAL KALEIDOSCOPE

First, some believe that human beings do not need either a supreme being or a book of sacred scripture to achieve self-fulfillment and a cohesive society. Allied with them, others fear that linking politics and religion, even if it favors their own beliefs, would deny religious freedom to others. Second, opposite this position, another holds that without a firm moral and religious foundation emanating from deity and sacred scripture, society's foundations will crumble. Understandably those taking this position desire to apply the precepts and tenets of deity and sacred scripture to such issues as education, abortion, sexual practices, clergy in politics, and so on.

These two positions—poles apart in their interpretations of America's past, their perceptions of the present, and their visions for the future—hold contrary views about the nature of God and of humanity and about what government should do and how it should be done. The dramatic divisions between the two positions spotlight important questions about public policy.

- What standards should guide the making of public policy in America?
- What standards should direct an assessment of the success of public policy decisions?
- Should the will or opinion of the people serve as the sole determinant of public policy and as an evaluation of its success?
- Or should an external reference point, namely deity and sacred scripture, serve as the ultimate authority?
- If society and government use an external reference point in making and evaluating public policy, who should determine and apply it?

Many maintain that American democracy should use ethical and moral measurements of divine origin as the ultimate guide in making public policy decisions and judgments. But what are those measurements? In the largely conservative Protestant culture of America's past, society and government could more easily reach consensus on this question. Ironically, in contemporary America such divergent voices as the National Council of Churches on one hand and the Family Foundation on the other have claimed to know what those measurements are.

Deep divisions regarding the propriety of our divergent moral and religious understandings tear us apart. Religion, once like glue bonding society together, now severs that bond. Competing on the same political terrain with nonreligious interests while trying to influence public policy, religious interests no longer function as they once did. Alexis de Tocqueville observed in the early 1800s: "In the United States religion exercises little influence upon the laws and upon the details of public opinion, but it directs the customs of the community, and by regulating domestic life, it regulates the state."[4] In today's pluralistic democracy, religious interests occupy a role no more exalted than any other interest. Secularization in American politics and society has generally lowered religious interests to merely another competing political force.

In legislative halls and courtroom chambers, a kaleidoscopic array of competing values and moral understandings divide Americans. Nowhere is this kaleidoscopic array more evident than in the following twelve questions.

- Should homosexuals serve in the military?
- Should the public schools teach both Creation and evolution?
- Should parents receive vouchers to send their children to private and religious schools?
- What financial aid, if any, should such organizations as the Salvation Army receive from the government?
- Should homosexuals have the right to marry?
- To what extent, if at all, should the public schools allow religious meetings and practices, such as Bible clubs and prayers before athletic events and at commencements?
- Should religious organizations have the freedom to determine their own standards for employees, including the right to prohibit the employment of homosexuals?
- What roles, if any, should religious leaders play in politics?
- Should public schools allow a moment of silence at the beginning of the school day?

- What limits, if any, should the government place on abortion?
- Should nativity scenes, the Ten Commandments, and other religious statements and traditions appear on public property?
- Should the government prohibit human cloning?

The issues are genuine. The emotions are passionate. The solutions are doubtful. And the reason? The American cultural kaleidoscope produces increasingly numerous and constantly changing patterns of moral and religious understandings, thereby increasing conflict and decreasing cohesion in society and, above all, raising fundamental and vital questions about the future of American culture.

NOTES

Epigraph: Robert N. Bellah, *The Broken Covenant: American Civil Religion in Time of Trial* (New York: Seabury Press, 1975), ix.

1. Michael Novak, *Choosing Our King* (New York: Macmillan, 1974), 114.

2. Aleksander L. Solzhenitsyn, *A World Split Apart* (New York: Harper and Row, 1978), 49, 53.

3. John Dunphy, "A Religion for a New Age," *Humanist* 43 (January–February 1983): 26.

4. Tocqueville, as quoted in Robert S. Alley, *So Help Me God* (Richmond, VA: John Knox Press, 1972), 21.

PART 1

RONALD REAGAN AND MODERN CULTURE

Ronald Reagan and Modern Liberalism

Charles R. Kesler

"The central conservative truth," Daniel Patrick Moynihan once wrote, "is that it is culture, not politics, that determines the success of a society. The central liberal truth," he added, "is that politics can change a culture and save it from itself."[1] Although there is wisdom in Moynihan's dictum, it suffers two defects. In the first place, it leaves unclear what culture is and where politics comes from—or to put it differently, it fails to put culture and politics in the context of nature, including human nature. Second, the statement is politically mischievous insofar as it implies that politics is the liberal vocation, and culture (whatever that means) the conservative one.

I suppose a liberal truth could be used for conservative purposes, and a conservative truth for liberal purposes, but Moynihan's sly association of liberalism with deliberate, salutary change—and conservatism with cultural determinism—is hardly evenhanded. Could a *conservative* use politics to "change a culture and save it from itself," or would that very endeavor militate against his being, or remaining for very long, a conservative? The dichotomy comes close to implying that liberalism's very purpose is to reform culture for the better, and conservatism's either to dismiss such efforts as futile or wait around for the chance to guard the new traditions faithfully. G.K. Chesterton drew the same implication, though from a different point of view, when he observed that the business of progressives is to go on making mistakes, and the business of conservatives is to prevent the mistakes from being corrected![2]

Moynihan's apothegm tends to turn the right either into apolitical fatalists who think culture is destiny, end of discussion, or into grudging custodians of liberal innovations, into Burkeans of a very dull sort whom only liberals could love. This, as it happens, is not far from Sam Tanenhaus's point in his recent book *The Death of Conservatism*. Tanenhaus, who edits the Sunday *New York Times Book Review*, criticizes contemporary conservatism as what he calls "revanchism" because it attempts a "counterrevolution" against liberalism, rather than sensibly accommodating itself to the enduring changes in American society since the New Deal. These changes, such as the growth of Big Government and the sexual revolution, were probably inevitable and at any rate are now unrepealable, he maintains; a political movement that doesn't recognize this is unrealistic and therefore unconservative. By seeking to impose various forms of political, economic, and moral "orthodoxy" instead of adjusting to history's dispensations, today's conservatives "seem the heirs of the French rather than of the American Revolution." They are Jacobin, not Burkean, in their political orientation, ignoring or rejecting the advice of sober conservatives like Whittaker Chambers (the subject of an excellent biography by Tanenhaus) to make peace with the elements of modern life that cannot be undone.[3] As William F. Buckley Jr.'s official biographer, Tanenhaus will have to square this account of conservatism with Buckley's own radical or anti–New Deal inclinations. If right-wingers are forbidden to stand athwart history yelling Stop, after all, what is left of the animating spirit of Buckleyite, that is, mainstream, American conservatism? Doubtless, that spirit must be disciplined by intelligence, and by a prudent regard to the difference between theory and practice, which means an acceptance of the truth that not everything can be improved that should be improved. Buckley was well aware of that. But from the imperfections of political life one should not conclude that the appeal to "orthodoxy," to permanent or ahistorical political principles, is itself heretical. Here is Edmund Burke himself on the point:

> I never govern myself, no rational man ever did govern himself, by abstractions and universals. I do not put abstract ideas wholly out of any question, because I well know that under that name I should dismiss principles; and that without the guide and light of sound well-understood principles,

all reasonings in politics, as in everything else, would be only a confused jumble of particular facts and details, without the means of drawing out any sort of theoretical or practical conclusion. A statesman differs from a professor in a university; the latter has only the general view of society; the former, the statesman, has a number of circumstances to combine with those general ideas, and to take into his consideration. Circumstances are infinite, are infinitely combined; are variable and transient; he, who does not take them into consideration is not erroneous, but stark mad—dat operam ut cum ratione insaniat—he is metaphysically mad. A statesman, never losing sight of principles, is to be guided by circumstances; and judging contrary to the exigencies of the moment he may ruin his Country for ever.[4]

Where do American conservatives look for their principles, for illumination of the proper ends of politics, for instruction amid the infinite circumstances of history? Ronald Reagan, the greatest modern conservative statesman, took his bearings from several sources, but most importantly from the American Revolution. Facing squarely the paradox that America, and thus American conservatism, starts with revolutionary action on behalf of certain self-evident truths, Reagan embraced those principles as coming from "nature and nature's God," not simply from culture or history, however much a culture was, and would be, needed to conserve and transmit them. His most significant speeches ring with these principles. For example, in the speech that launched his political career, "A Time for Choosing," delivered on behalf of Barry Goldwater's presidential campaign in October 1964, Reagan declared, "It's time we asked ourselves if we still know the freedoms intended for us by the Founding Fathers. James Madison said, 'We base all our experiments on the capacity of mankind for self-government.' This idea that government was beholden to the people, that it had no other source of power except the sovereign people, is still the newest, most unique idea in all the long history of man's relation to man." Later in that speech (which came to be called "The Speech"), he warned, "Somehow a perversion has taken place. Our natural inalienable rights are now presumed to be a dispensation of government." As president he pledged in his First Inaugural Address, "It is time to check and reverse the growth of government, which shows signs of having grown beyond the consent of the governed." And in his 1985 State of the Union address, after his smashing reelection victory in 1984, he made explicit what had been implicit in his politics all along, that he hoped to ignite a sort of second American Revolution. "Let history say of us," Reagan averred, "These were golden years—when the American Revolution was reborn, when freedom gained new life, when America reached for her best." He meant to change American politics, and by so doing change, or at least begin to alter, American culture. It might sound more conservative to say *restore* American culture, which is mostly what he had in mind. But to restore an unhealthy culture back to health is, perforce, to change it. The very notion of revolution, not to mention *founding,* implies that politics can change culture. A second American Revolution implies, like it or not, that politics ought to change not only many prevailing policies and political institutions but the habits of heart and mind that gave birth to them and were in turn shaped by them.

Mostly, however, conservatives don't like that bold notion, or at least profess not to like it. Conservatives of all stripes like to accuse the Left, after all, of "politicizing" our culture, imposing a tyranny of political correctness on everything from jokes to marriage laws. Libertarians start from the proposition that private life is both prior to and more valuable than public life and that economics and culture, as the characteristic, uncoerced activities of private life and, by extension, civil society, ought to be protected from political encroachment. Even so-called cultural conservatives, often accused by libertarians and liberals of wanting to use politics to impose their values on others, see themselves rather differently, as engaged in a long defensive struggle against secularist politicians who want to impose *their* values on ordinary Americans' practices of religious worship and expression, family life, and moral formation—the chief purposes of private life and civil society as the cultural conservatives define them.

Regardless of which wing of conservatism one considers, the typical conservative complaint is that what may loosely be called culture—religion, art, economic creativity and exchange, morals, science—should be ranked more highly than politics, and therefore as a general matter it should be shielded from political supervision. Whether students of Friedrich Hayek or Edmund Burke, most contemporary conservatives regard themselves as out to conserve the culture in the sense of the American people's evolved liberties, sentiments, habits, and ways of life. Politics will be necessary to this enterprise, but only as a means to a higher end.

However much good sense is contained in these reservations, conservatives should beware of talking themselves into second-class citizenship, according to which liberals would be free to change culture but conservatives duty-bound to preserve it. This isn't a fair or wise bargain for many reasons, as I've already indicated. It approaches cultural determinism for the Right, cultural license for the Left. And besides, conservatives like Reagan, at least, don't concede that culture is the ultimate consideration. There are good and bad cultures. Reagan tried to appeal to the best of American culture. Republicans, he said in his acceptance speech at the 1981 GOP national convention, were ready "to build a new consensus with all those across the land who share a community of values embodied in these words: family, work, neighborhood, peace, and freedom." He ended that speech with a moment of silent prayer and the benediction "God bless America." But the point of the "new consensus" was that the old one had frayed. Like Reagan, today's conservatives know that American culture has, in certain respects, deteriorated over the past decades. Almost all conservatives are keen to redress that decline—to instill personal responsibility rather than dependency on government, for example, and to encourage moderation rather than sexual will-to-power in youth—even if they disagree among themselves about what caused the declension and what government can do about it. Indeed, most conservatives respect our cultural traditions not so much because they are traditional but because they are *good*—that is, in keeping with human nature and happiness.

Culture, then, is a somewhat ambiguous concept. Etymologically, it derives from *cultura,* a Latin word meaning tilling or cultivating, as in "agriculture," the tilling of the land. The term points not simply to something that grows (as opposed to being made all at once), but to the action of growing something deliberately, with care, labor, and even reverence. The Romans applied the word, by extension, to education (*cultus animi,* Cicero called it) as well as to worship of the gods (*cultus deorum*). So culture is a people's unplanned way of life, the habits and mores that spring up from certain soils; but also the way of life deliberately planted and cultivated, typically by founders and legislators, among a people. For cultural anthropologists today (Barack Obama's mother was one, incidentally), every tribe or people has its own culture, by definition valid in its own eyes—hence "cultural relativism," the notion that every culture is equally valid or worthy. But at the same time, the notion of culture points to cultivation, to the *choice* of some practices and purposes as higher and worthier than others; and hence to the cultured or cultivated human being as the embodiment of the best practices and purposes—a standard by which to judge among cultures. In this sense, culture embraces both a people's way of life—something common to them and distinguishing them from other peoples—and the highest points of its way of life, which include but are not limited to what is usually called "high culture." In the best cases, those high points may be so grand and so noble as to show us something of what human nature is like at its best. One thinks of Bach, Shakespeare, or Abraham Lincoln—figures that transcend their native culture even as they glorify it.

So the disagreement between Reaganite conservatism and liberalism is not exactly over the politicization of culture. Each accuses the other of politicizing the culture, and each is correct, at least in its own terms. The difference consists of two different understandings of the political and the cultural. For conservatives, politics ought to serve ends suggested by human nature, hence, respectful of its strengths and weaknesses—always aware of the tyrannical passions in our fallen nature, as well as the portion of reason and virtue possible to man. "If men were angels," James Madison wrote, "no government would be necessary. If angels were to govern men, neither external nor internal controls on government would be necessary." Since government is "administered by men over men," both internal and external controls on it are needed, even as they are needed for human beings generally.[5] This view of human nature does not condemn politics to minimalist or purely negative functions, by the way. To quote Madison again, from just a few pages later in the *Federalist:*

As there is a degree of depravity in mankind which requires a certain degree of circumspection and distrust, so there are other qualities in human nature which justify a certain portion of esteem and confidence. Republican government presupposes the existence of these qualities in a higher degree than any other form. Were the pictures which have been drawn by the political jealousy of some among us faithful likenesses of the human character, the inference would be that there is not sufficient virtue among men for self-government; and that nothing less than the chains of despotism can restrain them from destroying and devouring one another.[6]

Thus conservatives who follow the common sense of America's Founders are keen for politics to show forth the capacity of mankind for self-government, to display and deepen the virtues involved in republicanism. To be sure, they know that politics must acknowledge and guard against human vices, must often supply "the defect of better motives" by dividing and checking the powers of government, separating church and state, and limiting government to tasks that imperfect human reason can evaluate and approve. But both to heighten our virtues and diminish our vices, conservatives seek to enlist the power of habits in the human soul, including the mental habits that Madison and Burke call "prejudices." In their own way, these internal controls help to elicit better motives, not merely to supply "the defect of better motives." For conservatives steeped in the Founding understand that statesmanship cannot be indifferent to character and culture: republican government needs a republican moral culture, not merely checks and balances, to sustain it. It is one of politics' jobs (though it is not always the *government's* job, because politics includes civil society and private efforts, too) to shape, nurture, and defend a culture that encourages good motives or virtues.[7] Among other things, therefore, conservatives second Madison's insistence on inculcating a *reverence* for law, and especially for the Constitution.[8] Neither governments nor cultures, they advise accordingly, should be changed for light and transient reasons.[9]

For the American Left, on the contrary, the tendency for more than a century has been to reject all notions of a permanent or essential human nature. In place of the old-fashioned view of man as an in-between being—between the beasts and the angels—liberalism has substituted the view of man as an open-ended being. He is defined not by his unchanging nature but precisely by how his nature has changed or evolved over the years in reaction to history's challenges. The most important aspect of human nature, in fact, is its very openness to change, its freedom in the sense of indefinite, and perhaps even infinite, adaptability. What we have seen of man's nature in the past is therefore not a good guide to what we may expect of him in the future. A new kind of idealism, based not on summoning the better angels of our nature but on eventually transcending that nature entirely, may take wing. As he comes to greater consciousness of his own freedom—his freedom from nature, in the sense of permanent capacities and bounds—man realizes that he is essentially not a natural or created being at all, but a progressive one, free now to take charge of his own evolution. He becomes his own creator, and the story of his development or self-creation is what many on the Left now understand as culture. In this vision, culture, conceived of as a product of *human will,* replaces culture understood as the cultivation of man's moral and intellectual endowment. And politics becomes the means of *transforming* man into a more perfect, or at any rate a later and more fully self-developed, being. ("Democracy," wrote the arch-Progressive Herbert Croly, "must stand or fall on a platform of possible human perfectibility.")[10] Neither politics nor culture is any more guided by nature and nature's God. Both creature and Creator, man becomes his own experiment.

Ronald Reagan wanted to reform American politics and thus, directly and indirectly, rehabilitate American culture. His political project aimed at four main goals: rebuilding American defenses and rolling back the Communist empire; freeing up the American economy; restoring national government to its constitutional limitations; and strengthening religious liberty and encouraging patriotism and virtue. Only this last point is usually referred to as Reagan's cultural agenda, but I think there were cultural implications to all his efforts, as one would expect from a statesman who sought a kind of born-again America, rebaptized, as it were, in the waters of the Revolution.

Of course, he was only partly successful. But let us remind ourselves of how remarkably successful President Reagan was. His administration precipitated the fall of the Soviet Union and its empire, which he aptly, and unforgettably, denounced as evil. His economic reforms kindled an enormous American economic boom that, spreading around the world and lasting almost two decades, discredited socialism everywhere. Even after the financial meltdown of 2008–2009, the Left in America and around the world offers no alternative to capitalism. We have heard populist grumblings, calls for smarter regulation, animadversions against bankers and politicians—but no hint that only socialism can save us. If anything, liberal politicians seem increasingly to recognize that only capitalism, however heavily taxed and regulated, can possibly pay for the welfare state. The financial meltdown has not even made American politics more liberal, beyond its immediate effects on the 2008 election. Obama was surely hoping that the economic crisis would trigger what might be called the New Deal effect, frightening Americans into turning to bigger government for more security. But as the Tea Party and the 2010 elections have shown, the effect has been very nearly the opposite.

The collapse of ideological Communism and the worldwide delegitimation of socialism are proof of the political sea change that Reagan helped bring about. "We meant to change a nation," he said later, "and instead, we changed a world." The change has a more explicitly cultural dimension, too, prepared by novels, memoirs, and plays by such writers as Alexander Solzhenitsyn, Whittaker Chambers, and Arthur Koestler, and beautifully captured in subsequent works of art like the luminous German film *The Lives of Others*. An ex-actor himself, Reagan played to the world stage, radiating confidence that if the Free World maintained its courage, the West would triumph and Communism, not capitalism, would be consigned to history's ash heap.

Reagan rejected the culture of despair that had seemed to settle over the country in the 1970s. Watergate, oil shocks, defeat in Vietnam, gasoline lines, double-digit inflation, high unemployment, Communist sallies into Nicaragua, Angola, and Afghanistan, American hostages in Iran—Reagan explained the decade's parade of horribles not as evidence of America's "inevitable decline" but of "mediocre leadership" that blamed its own mistakes on the country. "It is time for us to realize that we are too great a nation to limit ourselves to small dreams," he retorted. He began the practice of singling out "heroes" in his speeches and particularly in his State of the Union addresses, heroes who were ordinary Americans called on to do extraordinary things, often war heroes, but also citizens who performed more everyday but still virtuous deeds—individuals and families who served their local communities; and entrepreneurs with "faith in themselves, and faith in an idea, who create new jobs, new wealth, and opportunity." By celebrating entrepreneurship, Reagan set out to restore the moral respectability of businessmen and the life of commerce, which had been under political and cultural assault at least since Franklin D. Roosevelt had bragged about driving the "money-changers" out of the temple of American civilization.[11] Even as the New Deal had sought to drain moral prestige from the business class and transfer it to government regulators and bureaucrats, so Reagan tried to do the opposite. Liberals had tended to attribute business leaders' success to ruthlessness or sheer dumb luck; Reagan honored them as adventurers, brave risk-takers, and pioneers. As a result of his efforts and the amazing entrepreneurial wave of the past twenty years, the culture of the political and economic debate has shifted dramatically.

On two other fronts, however, Reagan enjoyed far less lasting success. Big Government and the so-called social issues defied solution and resisted significant mitigation. Although Reagan discredited socialism and ever-growing government, he didn't succeed in relimiting government along smaller, more constitutional lines. Here the welfare state and the modern administrative state proved too entrenched, modern liberalism's political and cultural assumptions too powerful.[12] At bottom, those assumptions rested on the acceptance of a new kind of rights in our politics. Before the New Deal, American politics revolved around the civil and religious liberties, based on natural rights, that one finds enshrined in the Bill of Rights and the Declaration of Independence. It was "to secure these rights" that "governments are instituted among men," according to the Declaration. Since the New Deal, however, social and economic rights—what we now call entitlement rights—have become increasingly central to our politics. FDR famously explained these as constituting "a second

Bill of Rights," implying that they wouldn't replace the first but were needed to supplement it.

Social and economic rights purported to make Americans secure, or at least feel secure, in a new age dominated by economic insecurity and depression. Roosevelt expected that the new rights—to a remunerative job, a decent home, adequate medical care—would render existing civil and political liberties, the offspring of simpler times, newly relevant. "Necessitous men are not free men," he liked to say. He meant that jobless, homeless, sick men are the stuff of which dictatorships are made. To avoid that fate, American democracy had to take care of a person's necessities when he could not do so himself, guaranteeing that he might live comfortably and fearlessly come what may. The immediate result was fairly innocuous, but the long-term result was worse because the *reasons* justifying even the most modest welfare rights pointed far beyond themselves. No one ever doubted that good jobs, nice houses, and decent medical care were fine things, which might well be the objects of government policy at some level. But the liberal alchemy that transformed these into *rights* was powerful magic; once unleashed, it proved increasingly uncontrollable. Such rights implied duties, after all, to provide the houses, jobs, and medical care now guaranteed to everyone. On whom did the duties fall? Liberals never came clean on that. They fingered the rich, who had plenty and so could spare to have some of it redistributed, but also the middle class, who could afford social insurance. Could benefits be cut or eliminated? Liberals breathed nary a word about such unhappy scenarios. They sold the new rights as though they were personal, indeed almost inalienable, not to mention cost-free—if not somehow a net gain for everyone. But in fact entitlements are positive rights, the offspring of legislative formulas that can be trimmed or repealed by simple majorities of Congress. And the benefits have to be paid for by *someone*—in reality, primarily by the young and the middle class. So the two bills of rights conflicted much more than Roosevelt let on. Which should take precedence, in short: Paul's right to health care or Peter's right to consent to taxes? Paul's right to a decent home, or Peter's right to property in his own home?

Yet the moral hazard of these new rights went further. Virtue was the way that free people used to deal with most of their necessities. For example, it took industry, frugality, and responsibility to go to work every morning to provide for your family. It took courage to handle the fears that inevitably come with life, particularly in old age. Confronting these unpleasant necessities on one's own or with the support of family, friends, and other institutions of civil society allowed for a certain pride in one's hard-won equality and independence. The new social and economic rights tended to undercut such virtues, subtly encouraging men and women to depend on government to rescue them and then to celebrate that dependency as true freedom. In fact, the appetite for the stream of benefits (the effectual truth of these new rights) promised by entitlements soon proved more addictive than liberating.

Behind entitlements stood a beguiling new version of the social contract—the "new deal," in the most sweeping sense of the term, that FDR offered Americans. As he put it in his Commonwealth Club Address (1932), government is based on a contract by which the people consent to lodge power in certain rulers on consideration that they, the people, be accorded certain rights. This formulation of the social contract resembles the Magna Carta more closely than it does the Declaration: rights are not natural nor do they belong to the individual; they come as dispensations from government. The people give government *power,* it gives them *rights.* This arrangement did not work out well in English history because the people often did not trust the government, and for good reason. Roosevelt and most liberals ever since have expected a happier outcome because modern government is not monarchical; it's thoroughly democratic, and they found it hard to imagine that a powerful democratic government would do anything undemocratic, anything that would contradict the will or infringe the rights of the people. Political tyranny, at least among advanced nations, they concluded, was essentially a thing of the past. Accordingly, government could grow big without endangering liberty. In fact, the more powerful it became, the more rights, in the sense of entitlements, it could grant. Here was the prescription for Big Government that Reagan fought against throughout his entire political career but could not quite overcome.

When government bestows rights, it doesn't have to bestow them on individuals as such. In fact, because the new social and eco-

nomic rights were designed to relieve necessitousness, to ease social and economic hardship, entitlements tended to go to suffering
groups, whose grievances could be heard the loudest. From the beginning, entitlements went to organized interests: trade unions, farmers,
school teachers, old people, sick people, and so forth. Little wonder
that such rights encouraged citizens to think of themselves and orga-
nize themselves into pressure groups—to indemnify their rights with
their group's self interest. These new rights were thus conspicuously
not attached to reciprocal obligations. The old rights were bound up
with duties. Your right to life meant others had a duty not to take your
life from you and that you had a duty not to take their life from them.
The new group rights, however, carried no specific, corresponding
obligations. At best, one assertion of right might check another. Old
people's benefits would have to coexist with school teachers' benefits,
and the groups would fight it out among themselves to establish a
kind of equilibrium, based on power, not right.[13]

Modern liberalism's success was not confined, however, to new social
and economic entitlements. It scored many victories on the cultural
front, along which Reagan and his administration also battled. Beginning in the 1960s if not earlier, liberalism made a crucial turn that
had a great effect on American conceptions of morality: from virtues
to values. The change in vocabulary was pregnant with great mischief
in our politics. In a kind of left-wing Cultural Revolution, virtue,
the idea of objective human excellence, was replaced as a focus of
morality by values—the idea that all moral judgments are subjective
or relative, reflecting nothing more than one's emotions, tastes, and
preferences. The term itself came into currency from Max Weber's
sociology (translated into English and widely circulated from midcentury on) and from Nietzsche's philosophy. (It had long been used
in economic and aesthetic discussions, to be sure.)[14] One of the most
remarkable facts about the reception of this new term *values* into our
politics is that it was soon co-opted by conservatives. The Right stole
the Left's word and began to talk about "traditional American values,"
although nothing was less traditional than that slogan, or "family values," although few families would have recognized the term hitherto.
Today one hears about the "values voter," a certain kind of social con-

servative voter. It's a strange phenomenon because while this term was adopted in order to oppose moral relativism, it assumes moral relativism. Reagan was an early adopter, but his sincerity in pleading for a return to "a community of values" could not supply the defect of his reasoning on the matter. If, as he would insist, all values are *not* relative, then those which are absolute or true cannot properly be called mere values. They are something else—truths, moral facts, principles, virtues. But not defending them as such tended to undercut the very argument he was trying to advance.[15]

By the 1960s students in most universities were familiar with the notion that all values are expressions of underlying passions, preferences, or will and that reason, social science, and even common sense are therefore disqualified as guides to right conduct. Radicals on and off campus, most of them quite well-meaning, concluded that if morals are grounded on emotions, then emotions can be a guide to morals. This is a form of what you might call sixties existentialism, in which the key to morality became the intensity of your feelings about the subject. The intensity of your feelings was in turn a measure of their authenticity, of the real *you* taking a stand for something or other—but at least for something rather than nothing. So the culture of the demonstration, of living for the excitement or the high of the protest itself, particularly on otherwise cosseting college campuses, became a characteristic part of sixties-style self-expression. When not demonstrating, the kids practiced the less strenuous existentialism of "do your own thing."

The sixties Left played at revolution rather than seriously attempting it, with a few exceptions like William Ayres. Why worry about revolution, after all, when history is already on your side? But when the Left's triumph ceased to look so inevitable—when voters elected Nixon in 1968 and again by much larger margins in 1972, when George Wallace consistently outpolled Eugene McCarthy— liberals experienced a crisis of confidence, fearing that history had betrayed them. Many retreated to the academy, to Hollywood, to nonprofit foundations, and to the unelected branches of government—to the courts and bureaucracies. Indeed, a remarkable feature of cultural liberalism from the 1960s to the present is that it has been pushed much more by unelected officials than by elected ones. From the early

1960s' Supreme Court decisions on school prayer and obscenity, to the 1970s' abortion cases, to more recent decisions on affirmative action, voting rights, and gay marriage, the most controversial parts of the liberal moral or cultural agenda have not been enacted by legislation but by courts and by bureaucrats.

In response, President Reagan called for constitutional amendments on human life, school prayer, and many other subjects. He wrote *Abortion and the Conscience of the Nation,* a graceful book arguing against abortion-on-demand. He appointed federal judges pledged to judicial restraint and the philosophy of "original intent," which Edwin Meese helped to spur as attorney general. But Reagan avoided more direct political combat over the moral or cultural questions partly because he had to worry about the Soviet Union and the American economy, and partly because of internal weaknesses in his own coalition. Libertarians were divided among themselves on the abortion question and united in opposition to several other items on cultural conservatives' wish list.

Cultural relativism or "postmodernism" continues to influence our politics today. In fact, its influence has diffused from elite down to popular culture at an alarming rate. One can even see it in the political assumptions and rhetoric of President Obama. You might expect this of a man of the Left who grew up in the sixties and seventies and spent ten years teaching constitutional law in the modern academy. Postmodernism insists that there is no truth "out there" by which men can guide their thoughts and actions. Postmodern liberals admit, then, that there is no objective support for liberalism itself; liberalism is nothing but relativism, to which a certain value preference has been added to pull it back from the nihilistic abyss. The leading academic postmodernist, the late Richard Rorty, called his version of this saving grace "the aversion to cruelty." A fully self-conscious liberal, according to Rorty, is someone who realizes the relativity of values but who is moved by his aversion to cruelty anyway. The corollary, by the way, is that conservatives are not very much moved by this aversion. They enjoy cruelty![16]

Obama is not a thoroughgoing postmodernist, of course, but neither is he an old-fashioned progressive. The typical "move" that postmodern thinkers like to make is conspicuous in Obama's writings—the move from truth to "narrative." We can't grasp truth or find meaning in some objective reality, claim the postmodernists; but we can create meaning by telling each other stories, constructing our own narratives—the more inclusive and empathetic, the better. President Obama often employs this language, as *Dreams from My Father,* his self-fashioning first autobiography, reveals. More importantly, he uses these concepts in speeches and political statements. For example, in his second autobiography, *The Audacity of Hope,* Obama writes: "Implicit in [the Constitution's] structure, in the very idea of ordered liberty, was a rejection of absolute truth, the infallibility of any idea or ideology or theology or 'ism,' any tyrannical consistency that might lock future generations into a single, unalterable course, or drive both majorities and minorities into the cruelties of the Inquisition, the pogrom, the gulag, or the jihad."[17] Implicit in the Constitution and the philosophy of the Founders, he seems to be saying, is that there are no absolute truths; because anyone who possessed or thought he possessed absolute truth would persecute in its name. "Truthers" would inevitably become fanatics of the jihad, the Inquisition, the gulag, or the pogrom.

It is certainly a good thing that America has escaped religious fanaticism and political tyranny, but no previous president ever credited this achievement to the Founders' rejection of absolute truth, previously known as "truth." What becomes of those self-evident truths that Obama's admitted hero Abraham Lincoln honored and risked all to preserve, and that Martin Luther King Jr. invoked from the Lincoln Memorial? Let us just say that Obama's wranglings with this question promise to be instructive.

In Ronald Reagan's farewell address, not as well known as it should be, he admitted by implication that he had not succeeded in bringing about a second American Revolution. He took proper credit for what he called "two great triumphs," namely, "the economic recovery, in which the people of America created—and filled—19 million new jobs," and second, "the recovery of our morale." By the latter he meant "the resurgence of national pride" that he had referred to, on several occasions, as "the new patriotism." These two epic achievements anchored what others called, he said modestly, the Reagan Revolution, which he defined as "the great rediscovery, a rediscovery of our values and our common sense." "I wasn't a great communicator," he said, "but I communicated great things, and they didn't spring full bloom from my brow, they came from the heart of a great nation— from our experience, our wisdom, and our belief in the principles that have guided us for two centuries." Yet in the midst of this *ave atque vale* he added a warning. The new "national feeling is good," he noted, "but it won't count for much, and it won't last unless grounded in thoughtfulness and knowledge. An informed patriotism is what we want." He recommended that Americans study their history and the political principles of their country. The "well-grounded" patriotism that Americans once absorbed from family, neighborhood, school, and popular culture is now neglected and frequently under assault. "Our spirit is back, but we haven't institutionalized it."

The future of American politics, in other words, depends on the future of American culture. Just as surely, however, the future of American culture, the reform of American culture, depends on the political and philosophical reappraisal of the modern state and modern liberalism. That reappraisal, beginning where Ronald Reagan left off, could mark the real beginning of a second American Revolution.

NOTES

1. Daniel Patrick Moynihan, *Family and Nation* (New York: Harcourt, 1986), 190.

2. G.K. Chesterton, "The Blunder of Our Parties," April 19, 1924, in *The Collected Works of G. K. Chesterton* (San Francisco: Ignatius, 1990), 33:313.

3. Sam Tanenhaus, *The Death of Conservatism: A Movement and Its Consequences* (New York: Random House, 2010), 16–23, 120. See also his *Whittaker Chambers: A Biography* (New York: Random House, 1997).

4. Edmund Burke, "On a Motion for Leave to Bring in a Bill to Repeal and Alter Certain Acts Respecting Religious Opinions," May 11, 1792, in *The Works of the Right Honourable Edmund Burke* (London: Holdworth and Bell, 1834), 2:474.

5. *The Federalist,* ed. Clinton Rossiter and Charles R. Kesler (New York: Signet Classic, 2003), No. 51, p. 319.

6. *The Federalist,* No. 55, p. 343.

7. James Ceaser says it well: "What is political in the broadest sense is not always exhausted by what governments are empowered to do, for what governments may or may not do is itself determined by the regime [i.e., "the way of life of society"] and constitutes one of its most important characteristics." *Liberal Democracy and Political Science* (Baltimore: Johns Hopkins Univ. Press, 1990), 73.

8. See Charles R. Kesler, "Culture, Politics, and the American Founding," in *Toward the Renewal of Civilization: Political Order and Culture,* ed. T. William Boxx and Gary M. Quinlivan (Grand Rapids: Eerdmans, 1998), 42–55.

9. Cf. Gary Rosen, *American Compact: James Madison and the Problem of Founding* (Lawrence: Univ. Press of Kansas, 1999), 128–41.

10. Herbert Croly, *The Promise of American Life* (orig. ed. 1909; Boston: Northeastern Univ. Press, 1989), 400. But if perfectibility is defined in terms of adaptability to the self's commands or urges, then the standards by which to measure progress become relativized. Over the past century, American liberalism has wanted it both ways—to create a new, demanding, universal democratic culture that is essentially a form of secularized High Protestantism, and to embrace multiculturalism, encouraging individuals and groups to be their authentic racial, ethnic, religious, and sexual selves.

11. Franklin Delano Roosevelt, First Inaugural Address, March 4, 1933.

12. See William Voegeli, *Never Enough: America's Limitless Welfare State* (New York: Encounter Books, 2010), 38–41, 203–4, 212, 217–18, 243–45.

13. See, for example, Irving Kristol, "Ten Years in a Tunnel," in *The Thirties: A Reconsideration in the Light of the American Political Tradition,* ed. Morton J. Frisch and Martin Diamond (DeKalb: Northern Illinois Univ. Press, 2010), 6–26, at 20–24.

14. Cf. Allan Bloom, *The Closing of the American Mind: How Higher Education Has Failed Democracy and Impoverished the Souls of Today's Students* (New York: Simon and Schuster, 1987), 194–216.

15. Cf. Charles R. Kesler, "The Reagan Revolution and the Legacy of the New Deal: Obstacles to Party Realignment," in *The 1984 Election and the Future of American Politics,* ed. Peter W. Schramm and Dennis J. Mahoney (Durham, NC: Carolina Academic Press, 1987), 245–64. See also Steven F. Hayward, *The Age of Reagan: The Conservative Counterrevolution, 1980–1989* (New York: Crown Forum, 2009), 638–39.

16. Richard Rorty, *Contingency, Irony, and Solidarity* (Cambridge: Cambridge Univ. Press, 1989), chaps. 3–5.

17. Barack Obama, *The Audacity of Hope* (New York: Crown Publishers, 2006), 93.

A TOUCH FOR FIRST PRINCIPLES

Reagan and the Recovery of Culture

Hadley Arkes

In the 1980s, in the days of President Reagan, Lou Cannon started a running line in the *Washington Post,* called "Reaganism of the Week." The insinuation here was that Reagan was speaking a version of what Mel Brooks would describe as "frontier gibberish." In other words, the president was simple-minded. Or he persistently missed the complications of the world as he reduced matters to things he regarded as rather simple or primary truths. Cannon offered once as a case in point an interview in which the president was asked how, as an officer under the law, he could support the Contras in Nicaragua when they were seeking to overthrow the legitimate government of that country. The president responded that it was indeed true that the Contras were seeking to take power at the point of a gun, in resisting the regime of the Sandinistas. But the Sandinistas themselves, he observed, held power at the point of a gun. And so, as he mulled aloud to the reporter, he did not quite see the moral difference between the Contras and what the reporter was pleased to call "the legitimate government of Nicaragua."

REAGAN MISUNDERSTOOD

Now the Gipper could not fill in the bibliography. He could not explain that his reflections here followed the paths marked off in the past by such writers on international law as Pufendorf, Burlamaqui, and Vattel. He probably could not have explained that his reflections here had led him back to the difference between an international law based on "positive law" and an understanding of international law influenced more fully by the axioms of natural law. By "positive law," we do not, of course, mean the opposite to something "negative"; we mean, rather, something that is law only because it has been "posited," set down, enacted, by the people whose edicts are enforceable as law in any place. When the positivist asked the question "Who formed the legitimate government of Nicaragua?" the answer came back without any moral ingredients: The legitimate government was the government that had effective *control* of the territory. That was not necessarily a government that enjoyed the consent of the governed. It could have been a Hitlerite regime, or the regime of Saddam Hussein. But if it were in firm control of the territory, it counted, in the positivist reckoning, as the legitimate government.

The alternative view, drawing on the moral tradition, insisted on the primacy of certain moral tests, casting up warnings before we would confer legitimacy on an exotic despotism or a group pretending to be a government in a distant country. That perspective reflected an older version of international law, because it reflected an older understanding of the connection between morality and law. The modern project in the law was expressed by Justice Oliver Wendell Holmes, when he famously hoped that "every word of moral significance could be banished from the law altogether,"[1] replaced with legal terms, nicely purged of any moral shadings. That state of mind has taken hold among many lawyers and professors of law, but not among ordinary people, for the connection between the logic of morals and the logic of law is inescapable; it cannot be removed. When we move to the level of a moral judgment, we move beyond statements of personal taste or private belief, and we begin speaking of the things that are more generally or universally good or bad, right or wrong, just or unjust—which is to say, right or wrong for others as well as ourselves.[2] John Stuart Mill observed that we stop using the language of "likes" and "dislikes" and start using the language of right and wrong, as we gauge whether someone should be praised or punished for what he is doing.[3] If we come to the judgment that it is wrong for parents to torture their infant, the next line is not, "therefore let us give them a tax incentive, or DVD player, to induce them to stop." If we think that torturing infants is wrong, we do not make contracts with people, or offer incentives; we respond with the moral voice of a command: a command that the torture cease. We forbid that torture to anyone, to everyone; we forbid it, that is, with the force of law. And that is essentially, I think, the classic connection between morality and law. It is the connection that Blackstone taught when he observed that the law was "a rule of civil conduct, prescribed by the supreme power in a state, commanding what was right and prohibiting what was wrong."[4] In spite of the best efforts of the law schools, that is still the understanding of law held by ordinary people, talking about these things with ordinary language. Ronald Reagan, anchored in the world and common sense, spoke about politics and law in that way, without knowing that he was speaking the language of natural law even after people in the law schools had stopped taking natural law seriously.

LINCOLN AND REAGAN

Lincoln had moved along a similar path, in his own understanding; and without knowing the bibliography, he managed to articulate a point made before him only by Thomas Aquinas. If we go back for a moment to that logic of morals, we understand that when we invoke the language of right and wrong, we are moving away from statements of merely personal taste or private choice. If we say that it is wrong for parents to torture their children, we mean to say it is wrong for anyone, for everyone, and no one can be legitimately free to choose it. Stephen Douglas, in his debate with Lincoln, professed to have no moral judgment on slavery; he was willing to leave people free in the separate territories to vote slavery up or down. He was, you might say, the first "pro-choice" candidate in our politics. But as Lincoln pointed out, Douglas had indeed reached a moral judgment. His position was predicated on the assumption that slavery stood in a class of things "not wrong." For if he truly thought it wrong, he couldn't hold that people were free to choose it. And so, as Lincoln famously said, "When Judge Douglas says he 'don't care whether slavery is voted up or down,' . . . he cannot thus argue logically if he sees anything wrong in it; . . . he cannot say that he would as soon see a wrong voted up as voted down. When Judge Douglas says that whoever, or whatever community, wants slaves, they have a right to have them, he is perfectly logical if there is nothing wrong in the institution; but if you admit that it is wrong, he cannot logically say that anybody has a right to do a wrong."[5]

There cannot be "a right to do a wrong"—it is one of those primary truths that becomes impossible to evade, and what is remarkable is that its relevance in our ongoing politics never ends. As far as I can see, in the tradition of political philosophy, only Thomas Aquinas made the same point about "no right to do a wrong," but Lincoln made it far more clearly and powerfully, perhaps because he was bringing philosophy down from the clouds to bear on the most vexing political issues that were straining our country at the time. In that vein, Harry Jaffa, in his classic work *Crisis of the House Divided,*[6] managed to bring out the ways in which Abraham Lincoln moved on his own along paths that had been marked out before him by Aristotle and Aquinas. And as one commentator observed, the accomplishment may be even more impressive when we know that Lincoln was not familiar with the writings of Aristotle or Aquinas. It might be said, then, that his mind moved naturally along the paths taken by minds that rank among the most impressive in the ages.

Without overstating these powers of reflection, I would suggest that something similar was at work with Reagan. He read widely, but even so he could not readily bring out, in his support, the writings of Vattel, Burlamaqui, or Pufendorf. The striking thing about him was that on his own, with his own curiosity in mulling over puzzles or moral questions, he often moved along paths of reflection that had been trod before him by writers more accomplished and celebrated in political philosophy. It is curious as to how this turn of mind went unnoticed even among journalists, such as Lou Cannon, who affected to have watched him closely. One of the most notable examples occurred early in Reagan's administration. The new administration seemed to be losing traction or faltering in the winter of 1981–1982, with a severe recession setting in. The political predicament seemed to be captured in a line making the rounds at the time: that Reagan's future, and the fate of his administration, would come to depend on where interest rates would be in the fall. That sense of things moved me to write a critical piece for the *National Review* in May 1982, which Bill Buckley played up under the title "A Lover's Lament for the Reagan Administration." (And the piece elicited a call from Reagan to Buckley, affably defending himself against a critique offered by a friend.) The cardinal point I put this way: How could it be that the standing and prospects of a conservative administration would hinge on anything as contingent, as wanting in moral significance, as the level of interest rates at any moment? There was a whole cluster of moral concerns brought together in the coalition that propelled Ronald Reagan into office—the aggressiveness of the Soviet Union, abortion, racial entitlements, suffocating taxes and regulations. No one who cared, say, about abortion would add an escape clause saying, "I'm voting for people who will try to protect unborn children from the killing of abortion—unless mortgage rates stay at 18 percent!"

Vintage Reagan

How, then, could we have come to a pass in which this sense of the larger things seems to have been filtered out of the public understanding? Someone had not been doing his job in cultivating, in the public, an awareness of the issues that truly mattered. The same point was amply confirmed from the other side: No Democrat intensely concerned with preserving "abortion rights" against the threat posed by the Reagan administration was likely to be won over by the news that the economy was now generating jobs at a prodigious rate, outstripping the creation of jobs in Europe (the experience that did set in after the Reagan tax cuts took hold in 1983). For people who were intensely concerned with questions such as abortion or the life issues, or virtually anything else in the issues of principle that divide the parties, the ups and downs of employment may matter, but they would not be decisive. On this question we will soon see another lesson, for we will see Democrats who will not cease voting Democratic even if unemployment holds stubbornly around 10 percent. Of course, not all of the public will absorb this sense of things, for many voters in the middle may indeed be voting for interests more prosaic and short term. But to make ourselves more alert to questions of principle was to convey, at least to the journalists and chattering classes, that we were not absorbing, for ourselves, *their* account of *our* politics.

In any case, this was my lament, and I thought I had a certain standing to lodge the complaint because I had worked with Anthony Dolan as a kind of consultant or helper with the speech-writing shop during the grand campaign of 1980. As I used to say, I wrote some of the best things Ronald Reagan never said. Still, I had a certain franchise to stay in touch, to kibitz and complain from the outside, as Tony and the crew settled into the White House. Not long after I had written my piece for the *National Review,* Tony invited me in for a lunch with the invitation to press my case or pour my heart out. In making that case, I cited a passage that the president had delivered in the State of the Union speech: He had noted that we give subventions, or subsidies, to people who lose their jobs as a result of competition with international firms. But he pointed out that we didn't give any such subsidies to people who lose their jobs as a result of competition with *domestic* firms. Out of equity, he suggested, if we did one, we should do the other. Yet it was evident that we could not do both. Therefore, he said, with a sense of equity, let us do neither. Let us simply repeal this lingering, vagrant effort to fine-tune the economy from Washington.

Now that, I pointed out, was vintage Reagan: It involved a question of principle; its rightness could be judged on its own terms; and that rightness would not be affected in any way by the question of where interest rates would be next fall. I remarked then: Find the guy who threw that line into the speech, and have him serve up about a dozen more. And by the way, who did write that line? Oh that, said Tony, "the President threw that in" while they were working on the speech.

Well, there we had it. As we used to say: Let Reagan be Reagan. His own paths of curiosity, his ways of reflecting about a problem, lingered with questions of principle, and he framed them in ways that were universally accessible. Rather similar to his musing about the points of equity in giving subsidies was his mulling over the matter of inflation. In his speech accepting the Republican nomination in 1980, he cited President Carter's charge that business and labor were making excessive demands, that people were heating up the economy and generating inflation by their own spending, with more money chasing a stock of goods that was evidently growing less quickly. But Reagan insisted that "we do not have inflation because—as Mr. Carter says—we have lived too well." And then he turned to that mode of musing about the problem: "High taxes, we are told, are somehow good for us, as if, when government spends our money it isn't inflationary, but when we spend it, it is." It is a line that draws us in and with a jolt delivers us from the haze of slogans. It leads us to look more closely for the real causes of inflation in the managing of the money supply.

In that same address I found him dealing with the passion of the environmentalists, determined to block the extraction of more oil at home, and he remarked that "we will not permit the safety of our people or our environment heritage to be jeopardized, but we are going to reaffirm that the economic prosperity of our people is a fundamental part of our environment." What was curious and striking about that passage was that it anticipated the argument that would be made more fully nearly thirty years later by Benedict XVI in the encyclical *Caritas in Veritate*. The pope pointed out that the Nature revered by the environmentalists was a nature purged of human things. We might put aside the question of whether human beings were in fact the culmination, the peak of Creation, in the biblical understanding. But it takes a certain perverse genius to conceive of Nature in our own day detached from the existence of those creatures who alone bear a moral purpose and can impart a moral purpose to inanimate matter. The beings, in other words, whose presence marks the existence of a moral purpose *in Nature*. But in the scheme of environmentalism we are constantly enjoined to save the Planet as though human beings were somehow not as much a part of that Nature as trees and rivers. In his encyclical, Benedict takes the occasion to drive home the gravest point that has eluded these people: The environmentalists seem serenely unaware that what they seek to do in the name of saving Nature may actually do damage to the integrity and character of "the human person," that moral being who is every bit a part of that Nature. And so, as Benedict writes,

> In order to protect nature, it is not enough to intervene with economic incentives or deterrents. . . . These are important steps, but *the decisive issue is the overall moral tenor of society.* If there is a lack of respect for the right to life and to a natural

death, if human conception, gestation and birth are made artificial, if human embryos are sacrificed to research, the conscience of society ends up losing the concept of human ecology and, along with it, that of environmental ecology. . . . The book of nature is one and indivisible: it takes in not only the environment but also life, sexuality, marriage, the family, social relations: in a word, integral human development.[7]

In the name of preserving the planet we may disfigure the character of human beings. And we can do that, in part, by inducing people to believe that they have a license to manufacture and discard human life to suit their own interests or advance a project in research, as though a human life had no intrinsic importance. We seek to extend the span of human life, while we gradually purge from ourselves any sense of reverence for those lives we profess to treasure.

THE TOUCH FOR FIRST PRINCIPLES

Ronald Reagan, of course, was nowhere near the world-class philosopher that Joseph Ratzinger is—a man recognized by the French Academy, deeply learned in the tradition of philosophy and theology, a man who works readily in Greek, Latin, and German. No doubt, he could fill in the bibliography in the way Reagan could not. And he could amplify the argument in a way that Reagan might not have had the reach to do. Yet what is so notable—and moving—here is that Reagan grasped the central truth of the matter. He grasped something that had eluded the environmentalists along with just about everyone else. He understood a simple but momentous point that people with intellectual pretensions far exceeding his own have not managed to grasp even yet. Otherwise, we would not have need of this beautiful instruction from Benedict XVI to awaken us to the point.

Plato recognized that the political man would need to understand what the philosopher understands in deliberating about the things that were just or unjust. But the political man also had to make himself and his measures acceptable to the multitude, composed of people who were not philosophers. The task, then, was to speak in a mode that was accessible. Lincoln said that the task was to impart the "central idea," and he gave us the most luminous examples of how that was done. Reagan had something close to that knack, I think, and it was combined with his touch for the things that ran to the common understanding because they touched primary truths. One of my own disappointments in pitching subjects for speeches was that I couldn't get my friends in the campaign to have Reagan do a riff on that striking example of natural-law reasoning that Lincoln gave us in the fragment he wrote for himself on slavery. He imagined himself in a conversation with the owners of slaves, putting the question, Why are you justified in making a slave of the black man? He imagined the conversation unfolding in this way:

> You say A. is white, and B. is black. It is color, then: the lighter having the right to enslave the darker? Take care. By this rule, you are to be slave to the first man you meet, with a fairer skin than your own.
>
> You do not mean *color* exactly?—You mean the whites are *intellectually* the superiors of the blacks, and therefore have the right to enslave them? Take care again. By this rule, you are to be slave to the first man you meet, with an intellect superior to your own.
>
> But, say you, it is a question of interest; and, if you can make it your *interest,* you have the right to enslave another. Very well. And if he can make it his interest, he has the right to enslave you.[8]

The upshot was that there was nothing one could cite to justify the enslavement of black people that would not apply to many whites as well. At no point in the chain of reasoning was there an appeal to faith or revelation. This was simply a model of principled reasoning; it was accessible to people across the religious divisions—it could be understood by Catholics, Baptists, even atheists. As Aquinas said, the divine law we know through revelation, but the natural law we know through that reasoning that is accessible to human beings as human beings. Or, we might say then, *natural* to human beings. And for that reason, perhaps, one did not need a college education in order to understand this argument. It was a model then of speaking in a manner that was commonly understood—and in a manner that touched primary truths, which were usually grasped at once.

I was urging a speech by Reagan applying that same mode of principled reasoning, addressed to the matter of abortion and running in this way: Why was that child in the womb something less than a human being? It doesn't speak? Neither do deaf mutes. It doesn't have arms or legs yet? Well, other people lose arms or legs in the course of their lives without losing anything necessary to their standing as human beings to receive the protections of the law. And the upshot was that there was nothing one could say to disqualify the unborn child in the womb that would not apply to many people walking around well outside the womb.

My own judgment was that this was the kind of speaking that quite fitted Reagan's style and that he could have delivered it with considerable effect. But, of course, Reagan and his staff had decided not to make abortion central to the campaign they waged in 1980 or any other time. To Reagan's credit, he sought to teach gently about this question of the unborn child, and he did it in that style of his by raising questions. In his radio talks he noted the first time he had faced the question of abortion, when he was governor. He was drawn by this curiosity: that the same legislature seeking to establish a right to abortion had passed a law making it "murder" to kill an unborn child in the course of an attack on a pregnant woman. He also noted that children in the womb already had standing to inherit property as heirs. And so he posed this question to his aides: Let's say a woman became widowed during her pregnancy, and she found that her husband had left his estate to her and the child she was carrying. Reagan asked, Would she be free to order the killing of the child in order to keep the whole estate for herself? "Wouldn't that be murder," he said, "for financial gain?"[9] Was Reagan not leading us back to the central question in the most engaging way?

The Danger of Dismissing Reagan

Steve Hayward, in his *Age of Reagan,* remarked on the tendency of those people in the class of public intellectuals—the writers, the academics, the people in the media—to dismiss Reagan as simplistic.

They knew, or professed to know, that life was freighted with more complications and nuance, as they say; that moral choices were never black and white, that there were always those shades of gray; that so much depended on mechanisms, administrative devices, modes of delivering services and getting the mix just right. But the problem, as Hayward recognized, is that people who relish schemes of administration may be tempted to absorb themselves in the details, while avoiding the moral question that lies at the heart of the thing. Edmund Burke once warned, in this vein, that refined policy is ever the parent of confusion. We've rarely seen a more dramatic example than the reaction of Hillary Clinton when Bob Dole, of all people, presumed to offer an alternative to that scheme of medical care that she and Ira Magaziner had managed to work out after long planning and the exertion of their administrative genius. Hillary Clinton remarked, with incredulity—and with no small outrage—that this plan offered by Dole had "never been tried"! Never been tried? The curious implication was that the vast, improbable scheme soon known as Hillary-care had actually been "tried"—that it had been tested somewhere. Had it actually been translated into operational measures, with all of the intricate interlocking parts and copayments and deductibles, and actually found, in experience, to be quite workable? Hillary Clinton and Ira Magaziner might actually have understood that intricate board game they had devised as a model for reshaping what was then 14 percent of the national economy. Richard Epstein noted at the time that the American Medical Association was having its meeting, spread over twelve floors at a hotel in Chicago, with specialists across the spectrum of medicine who could spot every mistake, every point of ignorance, in this scheme of bringing all of American medical care under central planning. But we can be virtually sure that Ronald Reagan would have listened to the presentation of "Hillarycare" and grasped at once that it was a scheme for a world that none of us inhabited. I want to make it clear that I don't discount in the least the kind of intelligence that permitted Hillary Clinton and Ira Magaziner to master the ingredients of that vast scheme they contrived for the governing of health care. I would simply point out that the intelligence manifested by people like Richard Epstein or Ronald Reagan reflected a different kind of intelligence; the kind we used to refer to as *practical wisdom*.

We often find our judgments hinging upon certain rules of prudence that may cut through the debates waged by experts on technical issues. Did the Germans have the technical capacity to build an atomic bomb during World War II? How far along might that project have been under the Nazi regime? Did Saddam have the technical capacity, with people rightly trained, to deploy weapons of mass destruction and build a nuclear weapon? But beyond these technical issues, there hovered questions of prudence cast in this way: If Germany under Hitler and Iraq under Saddam did develop these weapons, would Hitler or Saddam Hussein labor under any moral inhibitions or legal restraints in their freedom to use them?

At points like these, we also find a slight shift from first principles of moral judgment to principles of prudence joined with conjecture. It is one thing to say that it is wrong, wrong of necessity, to hold people blameworthy for acts they were powerless to affect. That is a first principle of moral judgment that will hold true under all circumstances and never fail to be true. But at times our judgments must be woven into conjectures about the movement of events, and they often turn on a reading of the character of other actors or the character of certain regimes. That was the kind of judgment that American statesmen were compelled to make when they had to guess whether a Hitler or Saddam Hussein would suffer any inhibitions, or want of motive, in making use of nuclear weapons. In 1948 most of agriculture in eastern Europe, in countries within the new Soviet sphere, was in private hands. Were those new regimes in Czechoslovakia, Hungary, East Germany, marking out separate paths to socialism, diverging from the Soviet model? Were they more independent, then, of Soviet control? Or were they as likely as the Soviet regime to distrust any critical parts of the economy under private control and not under the control of the Communist party? American statesmen bet on the latter proposition, and they turned out, of course, to be right. In the same vein, it seems to me, Ronald Reagan reduced one part of the conflict with the Soviets to this rule of conjecture: In a regime of arms control, the advantage tilted to the side of those who were disposed to cheat and who could be far more successful in controlling information and closing off the channels for leaks. That was the Soviet regime. It was a regime without a free press, without an opposition that could take power in a free election, without bureaucrats then who could leak information to the press and the opposition, and with no private lawyers to press cases in courts in which the regime could lose. But if the game were one of an arms race, the advantage tilted to the side that had the larger capacity for technological inventiveness and spirited genius, with a history of rewarding innovation. That was our side, the United States. Reagan bet on strategic defense, and he did it also out of a moral conviction that any national defense should truly be built around the notion of protecting the lives of our own people, not keeping them vulnerable to nuclear assaults for the sake of holding to a "theory" of deterrence that might never be tested.

The intellectuals missed both points—they were enamored of their deep-dish theories of deterrence and they regarded antimissile defense as a romantic delusion. It was not merely, in their view, that it wouldn't work, but that if it did work, it would make the world more dangerous by establishing American supremacy and threatening nothing less than the survival of the Soviet regime. In marked contrast to his critics, Reagan was more firmly grounded in his moral starting point, and he saw more clearly than they that his move to strategic defense could put the Soviet leadership under pressure and foster a crippling crisis in the Soviet regime. It merits saying, too, that he did not regard it as something baneful or implausible that the Soviet regime would implode, that Communism would come to be, as he said, but a "sad, bizarre chapter in human history whose last pages even [then were] being written."[10]

REAGAN'S PHILOSOPHY EMBEDDED IN JOKES

Ronald Reagan was of course famous for his knack of telling jokes. But the jokes were also part of his teaching, for jokes have a point, or they play off principles we count on people out there to understand. My friends know the argument I've made, that the comedians and the philosophers are often in the same business. For they may both make their livings by playing off the shades of logic and meaning contained in our language. And so, Henny Youngman would ask, How do you keep a marriage going for more than forty years? Twice a week, he said, my wife and I go to an intimate dinner with candlelight and wine. Twice a week we go: "She goes on Tuesdays, I go on Thursdays." Bertrand Russell used to joke about Mrs. Christine Franklyn-Ladd, who professed to be a "solipsist." That is, she professed not to know that there was anyone else in the world apart from herself. And yet she was so disappointed that she couldn't find other solipsists to come to a meeting of solipsists.

People haven't yet seen the real reach of Wittgenstein's observation that a whole system of philosophy could be conveyed through a train of jokes. And one thing that hasn't been fully appreciated here is that the laugh elicited from the audience is the surest sign that the point has been understood. The laugh is unforced, unfeigned, and it's the sign that people "get it"—they get the point. But what people may not see as readily is that the audience may concede, through their laugh, what they may not concede if the point were put to them explicitly in the form of an argument.

The best examples often involve the matter of sex, but I'll decorously put them aside for another occasion. I would recall, though, that moment in *Guys and Dolls* when Harry the Horse says that he has "5,000 fish" and that he's looking for action in a crap game. He is asked how he came by this "nice pile of lettuce," and he says, "I have nothing to hide: I collect the reward on my father." That line always gets a laugh, and the writers expected it to get a laugh even from a mass audience, for they expected everyone to share the sense that there is something deeply out of order—indeed, out of the natural order—in children turning in their own parents. The understanding reflected in the joke is the same understanding that Plato was surely counting on in the *Euthyphro,* for I'm sure he expected to elicit the prejudice of his readers against Euthyphro, who sought to have his own father prosecuted. Plato could play on that prejudice, even while Euthyphro is given, I think, the best arguments in the dialogue.[11]

When I say that the writers were depending on understandings planted deeply, it might also be said that they were depending on certain sentiments or passions quite natural to human beings, sentiments that we can find among humans across cultures. When I'm taking long drives, I listen to old recordings of my favorite radio comedy shows from the 1940s, the shows I knew when I was a youngster. Most notable here was Jack Benny. And what I find is that those recordings from the forties offer a kind of anthropological record. When we see where the laughs come and notice how surely and quickly—how quickly, that is, people grasped the point—we have a remarkably accurate picture of what the American people evidently understood in the vein of natural law at that time. And so, in one case, it is established that Jack Benny, with a bow and arrow, is a lethal threat. Phil Harris, his bandleader, bets Jack a dime—10 cents—that, with his bow and arrow, he can't hit an apple off the head of Don Wilson, the announcer. Jack, with alacrity, accepts the bet. That brings an immediate, loud protest from Don Wilson—he doesn't want to offer the target in that wager. To which Jack Benny says, Why are you so concerned? "It's *our* money." The laugh was instantaneous and massive. The point, of course, is that we can't risk human life for anything as trivial as a sporting bet—and a bet of 10 cents. I used to tell my students of the instructions we would give to babysitters when our boys were small. I'd tell them, If there is a fire, be sure to get out of the house that new manuscript of mine in this binder in the shelf just over my desk. "And yes—be sure you get Peter and Jeremy out." Something of the same point is engaged.

Now if all this holds, the premises are in place for something cutting closer in our politics: I have in mind that scene in a Mel Brooks movie, *The History of the World, Part I,* where the king of France, in the eighteenth century, is out skeet-shooting. The king yells "pull." At that moment a spring is released and what is thrown into the air as a target . . . is a peasant. Mel Brooks does not offer a sensibility overly refined. He has to count on the fact that people at large, in a mass audience, will get the joke. And the point of the joke is that we don't hazard human life as a plaything, as a form of recreation, no matter how useful the exercise may be in coordinating hand and eye. I would submit that when people laugh at that scene, or see the joke, they have essentially accepted every critical premise necessary to the moral judgment in a case running in this way: The young man, ever jaunty, tells his girlfriend that it's all right, we may do this for recreation and pleasure—I spill my seed into you, and not to worry: if anything happens, we just throw "it" away. That is how something once regarded as serious and even portentous in generating new life may suddenly be reduced to a matter so trivial that some among us will suffer not the least hesitation in throwing away that nascent being.

For Mel Brooks it was a joke, but when we understand the premises standing at the root of the joke, we realize that they are the premises that a large portion of our people have now absorbed; and once we see it, played out among ourselves, it may cease to be a joke. In one of my favorite lines, Red Skelton said, "They had a military wedding. Or . . . I think they had a military wedding. Let's put it this way: There were guns there." That joke is clearly the reflection of a culture that has vanished. It reflects a time when even the residents of Dogpatch, U.S.A., somehow didn't think they had a franchise to solve their problem through the simple expedient of getting rid of the child in the womb. There are no shotgun weddings any longer. And that is either because marriage is no longer regarded as a necessary framework for sex, or because a pregnancy may be ended now without forcing a marriage or altering the legal relation of the man and woman. If Red Skelton's joke can still elicit laughs, it is only because there is a minority who can still remember a shotgun wedding and even recall the understandings that lay behind that insistence, now seeming quaint, that a couple sleeping together should really be married.

That joke may be taken as a kind of anthropological fragment, a clear sign of a culture that has dramatically shifted from the 1940s or even from the 1960s. And that shift has been dramatically reflected in the altered axes, and the altered maps, of our politics. Bucks County in Pennsylvania, Nassau County in New York, Bergen County in New Jersey—pricey suburbs once reliably Republican, have shifted to become liberal Democratic enclaves. The division in our politics, and the class division there, is now a division not by income but by moral perspective. These are the divisions that mark the "culture war." In that war over the culture, the central issue has become the matter of sexual freedom, freedom from the moral restraints of the past: For many people, the "right to abortion" has now displaced the freedom of religion and speech as the first freedom. For these people, the right to sexual freedom is seen as the truer anchor of their deeply personal freedoms under the Constitution. From that core there radiates a cluster of issues, all connected: the destruction of embryos in research, gay rights, and same-sex marriage. And along with it comes the determination to resist the constitutional freedom of others to resist these new claims or even express their opposition: the resistance to gay rights may be stamped now, in certain places, as "hate speech" and may be prosecuted. The division here is on matters that really run to the moral root and to the nature of the human person—the question of who is a human being, whose injuries then matter to us.

REAGAN AND THE RECOVERY OF CULTURE

The task of recovering the culture is the task of teaching again the moral understandings that once anchored the culture that has been dramatically eroding. But we have seen moral recovery in the past, just as we have seen conversions in the past, conversions involving persons and then spreading to the rest of the society. And just as we have seen the sexual revolution since the 1960s, that revolution has begotten its casualties, its regrets, its deep second thoughts. What has changed before may change yet again.

The joke about the military wedding reflects a shift in conventions, marking changes of moral import. But the question is whether some of these jokes actually touch the things that will not change, the permanent things. My own hunch is that the Mel Brooks joke, about shooting peasants as though they were clay discs, will still be funny years from now, because people will still understand something as dramatically, even comically, out of scale in destroying human life as a sport or a plaything. But if I'm right, it means that we touch again those recognitions that cannot be extinguished, because they involve the things that are truly primary, the things that human beings are constituted to understand anywhere—wherever they happen to be.

Of course, certain things that we are constituted to know may also fade from our awareness. We may move along a path where we no longer recognize that we talk of discarding human life in the same way we talk about discarding trinkets that no longer please us. Or without quite noticing, we come to regard humans as less than human when they cannot live separately on their own, when they depend on the care of others. When Lincoln offered his fragment on slavery, and we recognized that there was no principled ground on which to remove black people from the domain of rights-bearing beings, we were being awakened to things we should readily have grasped. And when Ronald Reagan argued in the same way, the reaction was often "of course": he was alerting us to things we should have known, if only someone had posed the right question or framed the problem in the right way.

In the aftermath of Senator Scott Brown's election in Massachusetts, several commentators remarked that this is, after all, a "center-right" country. The Democrats, with a swollen majority, thought it was 1965 all over again, where they could reenact the surge of the Great Society with the expansion of the federal government in all fields. That surge followed the landslide victory over Barry Goldwater in 1964. And so let us recall that when Ronald Reagan stood up to give that speech for Barry Goldwater in 1964, the speech that launched his own political career, he was not standing up in a country that was understood at the time to be center-right, but quite the opposite. He was thought to be a voice at the far margins of our politics. Is it not in fact arguable that if we have a center-right country today, it is because Ronald Reagan taught anew some old lessons, in a manner that was accessible and appealing; that he taught us to understand ourselves, as a political people, in a different way, or in a way we used to be, a way that the intellectuals told us could never be recovered. But of course that older political culture was never irrecoverable, because the case for it was always there. And it was always there to be made anew by a political man or woman with the skill to make it in a way that ordinary people would still understand.

We are reminded, then, that the permanent things will not always be seen, that it is precisely the function of teaching—and of statesmanship—to bring them back to us, as in fact Reagan sought to do. We find ourselves backing again into the lessons of Plato's *Meno:* that so much of our knowledge is already tucked away within us, and it becomes a matter then of drawing out of us the things we come to feel that we have known all along. The genius of statecraft as teaching is that it reminds us of the things we used to know. And when it is done with the art of a Ronald Reagan, it also stirs the recognition that these are the things we have never ceased to know.

NOTES

1. Oliver Wendell Holmes, "The Path of the Law," in *Collected Legal Papers* (New York: Harcourt Brace, 1920), 179.

2. For the fuller exposition of this understanding, see my *First Things* (Princeton, NJ: Princeton Univ. Press, 1986), especially chap. 2.

3. See J.S. Mill, *Utilitarianism* (1861; reprint, Indianapolis: Bobbs-Merrill, 1957), 61.

4. William Blackstone, *Commentaries on the Laws of England* (1767–1769; reprint, Philadelphia: Rees Welsh, 1897), sec. 2, p. 44.

5. *The Collected Works of Abraham Lincoln,* ed. Roy P. Basler (New Brunswick, NJ: Rutgers Univ. Press, 1953), 3:256–57 (debate at Quincy, IL).

6. Harry Jaffa, *Crisis of the House Divided* (New York: Doubleday, 1959; Chicago: Univ. of Chicago Press, 1982); reprinted by the University of Chicago, with a fiftieth anniversary edition.

7. Benedict XVI, *Caritas in Veritate* (Vatican: Libreria editrice vaticana, 2009), sec. 51, italics in the original.

8. Basler, *Works of Abraham Lincoln,* 2:222–23.

9. Ronald Reagan, *Reagan in His Own Hand,* ed. Kiron Skinner, Annelise Anderson, and Martin Anderson (New York: Free Press, 2001), 380, 384.

10. President Ronald Reagan, speech at the annual convention of the National Association of Evangelicals, Orlando, FL, March 8, 1983. The speech can be found in the archives of the Reagan Library at this address: www.reagan.utexas.edu/archives/speeches/1983/30883b.htm.

11. But in that way, at the same time, Plato could deepen his argument in the most ingenious manner: If the best arguments come from the least attractive character in the dialogue, that may only confirm that the arguments carry with their own force, and not because of the attractiveness of the one who speaks them.

PART 2

CULTURAL CONFLICT IN AMERICA

THE FICKLE MUSE

The Unpredictability of Culture

Paul A. Cantor

And some had visions, as they stood on chairs,
And sang of Jacob and the golden stairs.
—Vachel Lindsay, "The Congo"

The sure way to predict the future is to invent it.
—Chinese fortune cookie

As an English professor discussing the future of American culture, I think of culture as meaning primarily "the arts." For the past two decades, I have been especially interested in popular culture, and I can say in all immodesty that I am regarded as one of the world's foremost academic authorities on *The Simpsons*.[1] Thus, focusing on popular culture, I will make the following predictions about the future of America. American cultural production over the next decade will increase at an average rate of 3.7% per year, topping out at 7.6% and never falling below 2.2% on an annualized basis. This overall growth rate will, however, mask a decline in the percentage share of motion pictures relative to that of television and video games. Motion picture production will peak in 2014 and thereafter suffer a precipitous decline, largely as a result of the simultaneous retirements of Stephen Spielberg, James Cameron, and Jerry Bruckheimer. By 2020 video game production will have outdistanced the total of motion picture and television production by a factor of two, culminating in the release of *Grand Theft Auto 27*, which will be purchased by every single person on the planet. During this same period, America's share of world cultural production will decline by 12.0–15.5%, depending on how quickly Shanghai software engineers are able to develop video games compatible with Chinese characters. On a more optimistic note: in 2020, *The Simpsons* will still be airing Sundays at 8:00 P.M., although the Fox Network will have long since been taken over by the federal government for reasons of national security.

These are the kinds of predictions Americans love to hear—complete with percentage figures accurate to one decimal point. Americans like to believe that the future is predictable, and in precise mathematical terms. Predicting the future has always been the dream of humanity and has kept legions of fortune-tellers, seers, prophets, astrologers, and the like gainfully employed for years. The astrologers of today are the economists, and we all know—often to the cost of our 401(k)s—how accurate their predictions are. Because we desperately want the future to be predictable, we assume that somehow it must be; therefore we listen eagerly to anyone who claims to be able to tell us what will happen tomorrow, or the next day, or one year from now, or ten. Since the world is simply awash with predictions, at any given moment one out of a thousand will turn out to have been correct, and we will think we have discovered the new Nostradamus. But the real test of prophetic powers is a track record; one successful prediction is almost always followed by a series of laughable mistakes.

TRUE AND FALSE PROPHETS

If we look at history, we see an unending succession of predictions that turn out to have been wrong, and that should teach us a healthy skepticism about the ability of the human race to foretell its future. This is especially true in the realm of culture in general and popular culture in particular, even in the short run. Big-budget movies that are supposed to be surefire hits routinely tank at the box office,[2] while every year produces "sleepers," movies that can barely get financing but go on to garner huge audiences and sometimes even Academy Awards. The record of long-term cultural prediction is even more dismal; the ability to foresee the trends that will govern culture in the future has proved elusive. Just think of all the Hollywood careers that were ruined in the case of people who dismissed the talking picture as a passing fad. We need to face up to the fact—culture is in the realm of the unpredictable.

To be sure, occasionally a cultural prophet hits the jackpot. Edward Bellamy, in his otherwise eminently forgettable 1888 utopian novel *Looking Backward,* correctly forecast the invention of the radio, which he cleverly called "the musical telephone." He predicted that music would be sent throughout a city from a central location by a system that would "offer a choice, not only between instrumental and vocal, and between different sorts of instruments; but also between different motives from grave to gay, so that all tastes and moods [could] be suited." Bellamy's prophecy was accurate right down to the details; he correctly foresaw that the music would be available twenty-four hours a day, and he even anticipated the clock radio, as one of his characters explains: "By a clock-work mechanism, a person could manage to be awakened at any hour by the music."[3] Cultural prophecy does not get any better than this, although it must be admitted that even Bellamy did not predict shock radio and Howard Stern. Some things remained unimaginable in the innocent world of the nineteenth century.

Studying the history of cultural prophecy thus should give pause to anyone trying to predict the future of American culture in the twenty-first century. Did anyone in 1900 have the faintest idea what the cultural world would look like in 2000? In the literary world, for example, did anyone foresee that by the middle of the twentieth century some of the most remarkable literature would be coming out of Latin America, Africa, and Asia? In the musical world, did anyone in 1900, with the possible exception of Arnold Schoenberg, foresee that within a decade composers would begin to dispense with melody and harmony as traditionally understood? In the art world, did anyone predict that artists would soon cease to represent the world in their paintings and that by midcentury two blotches of color on an otherwise empty canvas would pass for great art and be entitled to hang in any major museum in the world? More importantly, did anyone in the cultural world in 1900 even take notice of something called moving pictures, restricted as they were at the time to three-minute views of trains pulling into stations and the like? Above all, did anyone predict that this form of popular amusement would become the greatest art form of the twentieth century? Given the track record of cultural prophecy, I have to wonder how I, writing in 2010, can have the presumption to foresee what American culture will look like in 2100.

Physics versus Culture

I hate to play the part of the typical English professor and, as we say in my profession, interrogate the terms of my assignment, turning this essay into a metacommentary on the possibility of cultural prophecy. But perhaps we can learn something about the cultural future paradoxically by examining why it is impossible to predict it. And I want to insist on the point that the cultural future is unpredictable, not merely in practice, but in principle. This is not just a matter of my individual incompetence—although for the sake of argument I am glad to concede that point—nor is it a matter of our needing better data or sharper analytic instruments or larger samples or further experiments. We fundamentally go wrong when we invoke scientific methods and criteria of prediction in trying to understand cultural phenomena. Indeed it is the cult of natural science that has led to the cult of predictability in the modern world. Because physicists ever since Newton have been able accurately to predict the motion of planets, asteroids, comets, and other heavenly bodies, a general faith in the predictability of the world has developed in Western culture. This faith was shaken in the twentieth century within the world of natural science itself by the development of quantum mechanics and the Heisenberg Uncertainty Principle, and later by the rise of chaos theory and the study of nonlinear phenomena like the weather. But the success of modern technology—and above all its ability to make the trains, and then the planes, run on time—has continued to generate false expectations that the world is fundamentally a predictable place and that hence even cultural developments can be confidently foretold, as if artistic creation ran on rails.

Therefore we must draw some fundamental distinctions between the world of physical nature as studied by scientists and the world of human culture as studied by people like English professors. The planets whose orbits astronomers carefully chart are not themselves astronomers. Jupiter and Neptune are blissfully unaware of any claims we make about where they will be in ten of our earth years. But not so human beings, who have their own ideas about their future. In the cultural realm, human beings are making predictions about other human beings, and the predictees may well react to what the predictors have to say about them. Human beings are, among other things, ornery creatures. They might do the opposite of what is predicted of them just to prove the would-be prophets wrong. This may sound like a trivial point, but it goes right to the heart of the distinctive character of the cultural realm. In contrast to what obtains in physical nature, in culture we are dealing with self-willed individuals, who have minds of their own and may actually resent being treated as predictable.

In short, culture is a realm of free will, where the participants may change their minds at any moment and often act on whim. Culture is thus qualitatively more complex than physical nature. For one thing, cultural predictions may actually have an effect within the world they are predicting. We talk about self-fulfilling prophecies, but we might just as well speak of self-canceling prophecies in the cultural realm. Time and again, the confident and widespread claim that something cannot be accomplished has served as a challenge, rousing people to prove the naysayers wrong. All the people in the 1920s who insisted that talking pictures were a technical impossibility only served to ensure that someone would come along and make *The Jazz Singer* work later in the decade.

I have been studying the history of cultural prediction carefully, and I have come to one conclusion: cultural prophets will usually be wrong, because the people actually creating the cultural future are more creative than the people predicting it. This is in part an issue of age. The people who are asked to make predictions about the cultural future are authorities in their fields, and that means that most of them are old. But the people who are going to create the cultural future are, in general, young and precisely *not* authorities in their fields— they are going to challenge cultural authority. It takes imagination to prophesy the future of culture. But the people who will actually create the future typically have even more imagination. Hence the cultural future as it really emerges will typically surpass in novelty anything predicted of it.

To illustrate this issue concretely: ever since I set myself up as an authority on television, I am often asked questions like "What will be the next big trend on TV?" Or more specifically: "What do you think will replace *The Simpsons*?" or, not to sound hopelessly out-of-date, "What do you think will replace *Family Guy* or *South Park*?" I have a standard reply to such questions: "If I knew what the next trend in television is going to be, I would be out there creating it, and not talking to you in this classroom, where I make a lot less money than a TV producer does." This is admittedly a facetious answer, but it makes an important point. The people asked to make cultural prophecies, by virtue of being in a position of authority to do so, may well be the least likely to predict accurately. Precisely because they are authorities, they tend to be invested in the past and hence established patterns of culture. Indeed, they tend to read the cultural future on the model of the cultural past.

ACADEMICS AS CULTURAL PROPHETS

This is just another way of saying that these authorities are usually academics. Academics have perfect twenty-twenty vision in hindsight; they are, however, generally poor prophets. They can tell you that Shakespeare was great, and perhaps even why he was so. But they rarely can tell you where the next Shakespeare is coming from, if there is going to be a next Shakespeare (which, frankly, I doubt). Academics can be very good at analyzing aesthetic quality, but they are not as good at discovering it or recognizing it when it comes along, especially in unexpected places. They are in fact often among the last to acknowledge new developments in culture, precisely because of their role as custodians and conservators of the culture of the past.

This is particularly true when it comes to the development of new cultural media. Academics tend to understand a new medium by the rules of the established media, and they judge the new medium deficient by the standards of the old. To many academics, motion pictures for a long time looked like bad stage plays. By contrast, ordinary people began to realize that the motion picture was the new great art form of the twentieth century as early as its second decade. As we will see, some academics joined the mass audience in acclaiming these movies, but it was not until forty or fifty years later that the serious study of film entered the academic mainstream. This time lag may have had beneficial effects in the long run. It forced film to prove itself as a new medium in the court of academics and perhaps meant that when the academic study of film began in earnest, a sufficient body of excellent works had accumulated to facilitate the development of sound principles of analysis and evaluation.

Still, the record of academics with regard to the emergence of cinema as an art form does not inspire faith in them as cultural prophets. Like generals, academics often seem to be fighting the last culture war. They expected films to be like novels or plays and complained when films did not develop the interiority of their characters or did not obey the dramatic unities. When television came along, many academics treated TV shows as substandard films.[4] Academics tend to underestimate any new artistic medium precisely because it is not the established artistic medium. Because the history of culture since the nineteenth century has become bound up with the history of new media, academics have had a hard time keeping up with new cultural developments, let alone getting out in front of them. That is why I subscribe to *TV Guide*. With its links to the industry, it is likely to tell me more about the future of American culture than any academic journal of cultural studies.

It may be painful to give up our faith in the predictability of culture. But at the price of uncertainty, we should in fact welcome the unpredictability of culture, because it means that culture remains a realm of human freedom. The first thing many people say when they condemn popular culture is, "It's so predictable." They are referring to the fact that at any given moment of cultural history, the majority of motion pictures or TV shows look a lot like each other. They fall into recognizable classes or genres and seem to be produced according to formulas. Most cultural critics proclaim these formulas unchangeable, failing to notice that they are changing all the time, as various cultural factors, including audience taste and sophistication, inevitably alter, often quite rapidly. That is why most cultural critics do such a bad job of predicting the future in what they regard as the all-too-predictable realm of popular culture. The pop culture formulas are, as it were, snapshots that capture a particular moment of cultural development, but culture as a whole is more like a motion picture, moving along with abrupt scene changes. Because culture—even popular culture—is a site of creativity, it keeps eluding any simple formulas and continues to surprise us in sometimes disturbing but also delightful ways.

A Case Study of Cultural Prophecy

Having totally undermined any credibility I might have had as a cultural prophet, I will nevertheless pursue my assigned task by means of a single case study of predicting the cultural future in America. Perhaps the best way to get a handle on the cultural future is to turn to the past and see how cultural predictions have fared historically. By that means we can develop a sense of what typically can go wrong in cultural predictions, and especially determine the biases and blind spots cultural prophets tend to suffer from. I will deal with a truly remarkable example of cultural prophecy, a book that was published in 1915 called *The Art of the Moving Picture*, by Vachel Lindsay. Lindsay was a minor American poet who is almost totally forgotten today. I knew of him only because of his poem "The Congo," which I remember being taught in high school in the late 1950s. Lindsay's book on the moving picture is also unknown to the general public. Film historians acknowledge it to be among the first books—if not the very first—in America to deal seriously with the cinema, and indeed, it is one of the first such books published anywhere in the world.[5] *The Art of the Moving Picture* offers a strange combination of penetrating intelligence and downright wackiness. At moments, Lindsay displays truly extraordinary insights into the nature of film as a distinct medium and offers predictions for its future that turn out to have been uncannily accurate. But Lindsay also makes dubious pronouncements about motion pictures and their future, suggesting that he is completely misunderstanding the medium and has no idea where it is heading. Lindsay's book is accordingly a good lesson in cultural prophecy; at times it can restore one's faith in the possibility of foreseeing the cultural future, but at other times it can serve as a warning against the pitfalls of trying to outguess the creative forces in a new medium.

To illustrate the wacky side of Lindsay's book, I can cite one of his many rules for interpreting the visual symbolism of movies: "Nothing very terrible can happen with a duck in the foreground. . . . It would take Maeterlinck or Swedenborg to find the mystic meaning of a duck. A duck looks to me like a caricature of an alderman."[6] This is Lindsay at his most idiosyncratic, but unfortunately it is not wholly atypical of the book. More seriously, Lindsay was one of the many who were convinced that the motion picture is in its very essence a silent medium. Thus he did not simply doubt the technical feasibility of talking pictures; he was certain that spoken dialogue would spell the ruin of cinema as an art form. Convinced that movies would forever remain silent, Lindsay concluded that audiences did not have to be. He devotes a chapter to arguing that people should discuss movies while watching them. He does not just say that they should be allowed to do so; he wants the management actively to encourage talking during movies, albeit at low volume. One wonders whether, if Lindsay were alive today, he would advocate the use of cell phones in movie theaters to spread the conversation beyond their walls.

But side-by-side with notions that seem misguided if not laughable to us today, Lindsay can take one's breath away with his prophetic power. For example, among all the cinema talent available to him, he singles out the Japanese-American actor-director Sessue Hayakawa. Today Hayakawa is remembered mainly for his role as Colonel Saito in the 1957 film *The Bridge on the River Kwai,* for which he was nominated for an Oscar for Best Supporting Actor. Few people are aware that Hayakawa was one of the biggest stars of the silent era in Hollywood. With Lindsay's training in the fine arts, especially painting, he was perceptive enough to detect something oriental in Hayakawa's films: "He looks like all the actors in the old Japanese prints" (64). Accordingly, Lindsay called upon Hayakawa to stop playing orientalist stereotypes like Japanese spies (65) and instead to bring authentic Japanese material to the screen: "Sessue Hayakawa should give us Japanese tales more adapted to films. We should have stories of Iyeyasu and Hideyoshi, written from the ground up for the photoplay theatre. We should have the story of the Forty-seven Ronin. . . . We should have legends of the various clans, picturizations of the code of the Samurai" (81).

Writing in 1915, Lindsay manages to predict the film masterpieces of the great Japanese director Akira Kurosawa, as well as several outstanding Japanese film versions of the Chushingura story, or, as it is also known, the tale of the forty-seven Ronin, made by other Japanese directors.[7] It is as if someone writing in Britain in 1562 (two years before the birth of Shakespeare) had just witnessed a performance of *Gorboduc* (the first blank-verse tragedy in English) and predicted: "This is a powerful new medium; I just wish a playwright would do more with British history and create dramas about, say, King Lear or Macbeth." Lindsay's performance as a cinematic prophet is even more amazing, because he had to step outside Western culture and see that the cinema is a world art form and could be adapted to oriental material. To be sure, Hayakawa himself never fulfilled Lindsay's prophecy,[8] but roughly forty years later Kurosawa embarked on a series of samurai films that are among the glories of world cinema. And the one I regard as his greatest film—*Kagemusha* (1980)—is based on the story of the very Iyeyasu Lindsay recommended to Hayakawa as a subject for a film.[9]

In assessing Lindsay as a cultural prophet, we can begin with the simple fact that he was writing a book on the art of the moving picture at all in 1915—that is, at a time when virtually all cultural authorities dismissed movies as a low form of popular entertainment, if they even deigned to note their existence in the first place. One can argue that this was the earliest possible moment when such a book could have been written with any degree of plausibility. In 1915 evidence was at hand for the first time that the motion picture could be a genuine art form. Giovanni Pastrone's *Cabiria*, a movie about the struggle between Rome and Carthage, had come out in Italy in 1914 and had just been released in the United States, and of course D.W. Griffith's *The Birth of a Nation* had just created perhaps the greatest sensation that any film ever has. Many film critics today would say that these two are the first truly great films in movie history.[10] They are both epic in subject matter and in length (each ran for roughly three hours, depending on the cut), and they both pushed the existing limits of the cinematic art, introducing, for example, new camera techniques. And Lindsay managed to proclaim these films as artistic masterpieces at just the moment they came out.[11]

This kind of immediate recognition of a turning point in culture is very rare in the history of art criticism. To draw roughly the same analogy again, it is as if someone in 1588 viewed the first great Elizabethan play—Christopher Marlowe's *Tamburlaine*—and on the spot proclaimed the dawn of a great new era in popular theater in England. Lindsay himself draws this parallel. Faced with Griffith's towering achievement in his movie *Intolerance*, Lindsay pulls out all the stops in his praise: "Griffith is, in Intolerance, the ungrammatical Byron of the films, but certainly as magnificent as Byron, and since he is the first of his kind, I, for one, am willing to name him with Marlowe" (11). D.W. Griffith as the Christopher Marlowe of the motion picture sounds exactly right to me. Just as Marlowe did in the Elizabethan theater, Griffith in the motion picture industry was the first to reveal the full artistic potential of the new medium, while at the same time scoring an unprecedented and unparalleled commercial success.

Mentioning *Intolerance* requires a quick scholarly digression. *Intolerance* came out in 1916; I have said that Lindsay's book was published in 1915. I am claiming prophetic powers for Lindsay, but not the preternatural ability to analyze a film before he could have seen it. Discussion of *The Art of the Moving Picture* is slightly complicated by the fact that it came out in a second edition in 1922. But the bulk of the book, even as we have it in the 1922 edition, was written in 1915, and one can always be sure that a discussion of a post-1915 film was written for the 1922 publication.[12] Frankly, the book would still be remarkably prophetic even if all of it had been written in 1922. And Lindsay did not waste the additional years at his disposal as an analyst. One of the films he adds to his list of cinematic classics in the 1922 edition is the early masterpiece of German expressionist cinema, the 1920 *Cabinet of Dr. Caligari*. Already in 1922, Lindsay is making insightful comments about this epoch-making film: "The cabinet of Dr. Caligari is indeed a cabinet, and the feeling of being in a cell, and smothered by all the oppressions of a weary mind does not desert the spectator for a minute. . . . It proves in a hundred ways the resources of the film" (8). What I find so extraordinary is the way Lindsay—writing just when these films were being released—singles out as masterpieces precisely the works that film critics to this day hold up as triumphs of the silent era: *Cabiria, The Birth of a Nation, Intolerance,*

The Cabinet of Dr. Caligari. In the long history of criticism in the arts, one would find few examples of a critic displaying comparable foresight, especially when dealing with works produced in the earliest years of a new medium's development.

Forming the Cultural Canon

To be sure, Lindsay praises many works that do not appear today on anybody's list of the one hundred greatest movies of all time. Sometimes the movies he talks about simply no longer exist. Reading the book is like a voyage to the Island of Lost Reels, a glimpse into the forgotten past of cinema, as the credits roll by: *Such a Little Tree, What the Daisy Said, Neptune's Daughter, Oil and Water, The Mine Owner's Daughter,* and two of the more provocative titles, *The Wild Girl of the Sierras* and (my personal favorite) *The Land of the Head Hunters.* For all I know, some of these may be significant cinematic achievements and may even be available somewhere on DVD. I did check, however, and none of these titles appear in two of the most comprehensive histories of film, David Shipman's *The Story of Cinema* and David Cook's *A History of Narrative Film* (each book is more than one thousand pages long, and Shipman's is double-columned).[13] It is a sobering experience to realize that films that Lindsay values highly and holds up as models of the art have disappeared entirely. It is like finding the names of the lost plays of Aeschylus, Sophocles, Euripides, and Aristophanes in ancient chronicles, or even the names of playwrights like Agathon, of whose output only the smallest fragments have survived. We would do well to remember that our view of the cultural future is inevitably shaped by our understanding of the cultural past, and our knowledge of that past is incomplete. What we have of the past—even a past as recent as the first two decades of the twentieth century—is partly the result of accidental factors, like the burning of the Library of Alexandria in the ancient world or the degeneration of film stock in the modern world. Much that we value in our culture today may well be lost as well at some point in the future.

Lindsay waxes particularly eloquent about another film that has evidently been lost: *The Battle Hymn of the Republic.*[14] He calls it one of "the two most significant photoplays I have ever encountered" (86;

the other is Griffith's reasonably well-known 1914 *Judith of Bethulia*).[15] Lindsay admits that *Battle Hymn* "may have many technical crudities by present-day standards," but still he insists: "Every student of American Art should see this film" (105). Already in 1915 Lindsay is involved in what we call canon formation. He says of *Battle Hymn*: "This film should be studied in the High Schools and Universities till the canons of art for which it stands are established in America" (101). Lindsay is trying to determine which films represent the cinematic art at its best and which therefore serve to reveal its nature. It is the same task Aristotle set himself with regard to Greek drama in his *Poetics*. Lindsay is acutely aware that he is observing the birth of a new medium and claims that his commentary is particularly significant for just that reason (while also showing his awareness of the fragility of the new medium of film): "There can never be but one first of anything, and if the negatives of these films survive the shrinking and the warping that comes with time, they will still be, in a certain sense classics" (1). Lindsay takes great pride in his pioneering efforts to shape the cinematic canon: "And the lists of films given in books two and three of this work are the only critical and carefully sorted lists of the early motion pictures that I happen to know anything about" (2).

We must remember that Lindsay was writing at a time when most people thought of films as simply disposable, something to give audiences a moment's pleasure and then be seen no more. Lindsay shows his foresight in the way he assumes that film would become an art for the ages. He accurately predicts that films would eventually be archived: "There will be available at certain centres collections of films equivalent to the Standard Dictionary and the Encyclopædia Britannica" (253). Without exactly foreseeing the videocassette or the DVD, he did look forward to the ready availability of movies in people's homes: "Photoplay libraries are inevitable, as active if not as multitudinous as the book-circulating libraries" (254). Admittedly, Lindsay failed to foresee Blockbuster or Netflix, but for someone writing in 1915, he deserves credit just for realizing that films were not throwaway items but would have lasting value and be recycled endlessly in various forms of reproduction. At least *The Birth of a Nation* was preserved, though evidently not *The Land of the Head Hunters*.

And here we come to the pitfalls of instantaneous canon formation. We are duly impressed by Lindsay's ability to identify cinematic classics at the moment they appeared, but we must also be troubled by his tendency to get carried away by what look to us in retrospect like momentary enthusiasms. He evidently ranks the never-to-be-forgotten *Birth of a Nation* below the long-since-forgotten *Battle Hymn of the Republic.* This is a good reminder that contemporary criticism is likely to be uneven and inconsistent. A sharp critic may be able to spot the masterpieces being created in his own day, but he is also likely to mistake what turn out to have been passing fads for lasting artistic contributions. That is why the test of time is crucial to the process of canon formation; it may take years to sort out the wheat from the chaff, and no one critic can perform the task alone. That is also one reason why criticism works better as a retrospective than a predictive science. If we try to infer the future from the present, we are likely to go wrong precisely because we need the future to find out what really is important and of long-lasting significance in our own day. Paradoxically, rather than the present being a clue to the future, the future may be our best clue to the present.

Notice that Lindsay gets the canon neither all right nor all wrong. One common view is that an artistic genius is never recognized by his contemporaries because his work is too revolutionary. Endlessly recycling the story of the audience riot at the debut of Stravinsky's *Rite of Spring,* cultural elitists insist that an artist proves his greatness precisely by displeasing his contemporaries. Lindsay's book provides a useful corrective to this cultural myth. *The Birth of a Nation* is a work of cinematic genius and a revolutionary movie if there ever were one. And yet it was a critical and commercial success right from the beginning (although, because of its racism, it generated a great deal of controversy at the time and has done so ever since). But we should not go to the opposite extreme of believing that artists' contemporaries are always good judges of their work. As in all the other arts, cinematic history is filled with cases of works that were misjudged and rejected when they first came out and only later were rediscovered and recognized as the masterpieces they truly are.

By the same token, as the example of *Battle Hymn* in Lindsay suggests, some movies turn out to have been wildly overrated by contemporaries, for personal or other idiosyncratic reasons. The religious element in *Battle Hymn* seems to be what ultimately provoked Lindsay's extravagant praise: "The celestial company, its imperceptible emergence, its spiritual power when in the ascendant, is a thing never to be forgotten, a tableau that proves the motion picture a great religious instrument" (103). Critics have always allowed nonaesthetic factors to influence what are supposed to be purely aesthetic judgments of value. There are several points in *The Art of the Moving Picture* where Lindsay lets his religious beliefs determine how high he rates a particular movie. As brilliant as the book is in predicting which of the early films would live on to become classics, Lindsay's overenthusiasm for some films is a good lesson in how even the most acute critic can allow his personal feelings to cloud his judgment.

Cultural Turning Points

I have by no means exhausted Lindsay's insights into cinema in the days of its infancy. For example, long before the widespread practice of celebrity product endorsement, he divined the advertising potential of the movies: "Some staple products will be made attractive by having film-actors show their uses" (253). Lindsay seems to be talking about the way movies can be used to demonstrate products, but he also has an inkling of how to employ pure star power to sell merchandise. More impressively, Lindsay really has a grasp of the big picture and explicitly states that he is writing about one of the great turning points in cultural history, one of the epochal shifts in media. That explains one of the most surprising aspects of *The Art of the Moving Picture*—the fact that Lindsay devotes a long chapter to, of all subjects, Egyptian hieroglyphics. He solemnly instructs the fledgling moviemaker: "Let the man searching for tableau combinations, even if he is of the practical commercial type, prepare himself with eight hundred signs from Egypt" (200). When trying to understand the art of the future, it does not seem promising to begin by going back to 2000 BCE and the land of the pharaohs.

But Lindsay's seemingly inappropriate discussion of hieroglyphics turns out to be one of the ways in which he brilliantly anticipates later media prophets, including Marshall McLuhan. In understanding the epochal novelty of film as a medium, Lindsay views it as a way of overcoming the preceding era of print and in that sense a return to an earlier medium: "The invention of the photoplay is as great a step as was the beginning of picture-writing in the stone age. And the cave-men and women of our slums seem to be the people most affected by this novelty, which is but an expression of the old in that spiral of life which is going higher while seeming to repeat the ancient phase" (199). Lindsay's seemingly offensive description of poor people as "cave-men and women" is just his way of saying that they cannot read, and indeed the new art of motion pictures appealed particularly to the illiterate in America, specifically the huge number of immigrants who were flocking to its shores in the early twentieth century. They did not understand English, but they were able to understand the cinema, because it tells stories in the universal language of pictures.

Long before McLuhan and other media pundits, Lindsay is suggesting that, with the coming of film, America may be entering a postliterate phase of culture and that one way of understanding it may be to look at preliterate cultures. Lindsay's image of the spiral is pure McLuhan—to advance beyond the era of alphabetic and print culture, we have to circle back to what preceded it. Lindsay's invocation of Egyptian hieroglyphics is thus not as crazy as it may at first seem. He is searching in ancient Egyptian culture for a way of breaking out of the alphabetic, literate mode and learning to think again in pictures: "It would profit any photoplay man to study to think like the Egyptians, the great picture-writing people" (200–201). After all, Lindsay thinks of film as the art of the moving *picture*. Thus he regards studying hieroglyphics as a way to break the habit ingrained by print culture of thinking in terms of words and to start thinking anew in pictorial images.[16] In terms that truly anticipate McLuhan, Lindsay writes: "Edison is the new Gutenberg. He has invented the new printing. The state that realizes this may lead the soul of America, day after to-morrow" (252).

CALIFORNIA HERE WE COME

Here Lindsay introduces a new issue and shows his understanding of the larger context of cultural developments, their economic, social, and even political implications. *The Art of the Moving Picture* has an entire chapter called "California and America." Lindsay was quick to grasp the broader significance of the fact that by 1915 the American movie industry had largely migrated from the New York–New Jersey area where it originated to Los Angeles and its environs. Lindsay understood that this move was made largely because of the requirements of outdoor filming—the quest for reliable good weather—as well as the availability of a wide variety of landscapes in the immediate vicinity of Los Angeles to serve as backdrops for films. But Lindsay sensed that something deeper was happening, a shift in American cultural geography. At a time when the Dodgers were still in Brooklyn and the Giants in New York, he correctly intuited that the balance of power between the East Coast and the West Coast was finally tilting toward the Pacific.[17]

Elsewhere in the book Lindsay argues that the art of the moving picture will develop regionally in the United States. Indeed he hopes that it will lead to the flourishing of a new regionalism in American culture. He advocates the making of films locally, and speculates that any good-sized American city should be able to draw upon existing theater resources to produce its own films for local consumption. Because, like many, he already associated Hollywood with commercial moviemaking, he resisted its growing dominance of film production and the emerging national scale of the movie market. At one of the few points where he explicitly adopts a prophetic voice, he gets the future completely wrong: "So I prophesy . . . Santa Fe is the artistic, architectural, and song capital at this hour. And I hope it may become the motion picture capital of America from the standpoint of pure art, not manufacture" (26).

This turned out to be wishful thinking on Lindsay's part, but he shows signs of knowing full well that the future of cinema lay in Hollywood: "California indeed stands a chance to achieve through the films an utterance of her own. Will this land furthest west be the first to capture the inner spirit of this newest and most curious of the arts?" (246). Lindsay realizes how much is at stake in the question of whether one locale will dominate the movie business. He talks about the long-standing dominance of Boston in American culture: "Patriotic art students have discussed with mingled irony and admiration the Boston domination of the only American culture of the nineteenth century, namely literature. . . . Boston still controls the text-book in English and dominates our high schools" (246–47). Lindsay wants to see the cultural domination of Boston broken: "Some of us view with a peculiar thrill the prospect that Los Angeles may become the Boston of the photoplay" (247). In retrospect, we can see that Lindsay was right to think that shifting the cultural center of America from Boston to Los Angeles would be quite a revolution. It is just that many have viewed that prospect not with "a peculiar thrill" but with a peculiar horror.

In fact, even though Lindsay likes the idea of breaking the East Coast's cultural hegemony, he had the good sense to worry about what would happen if Los Angeles, and California more generally, became the standard-bearer of American culture. He celebrates the broad horizons of the state but wonders if people might get lost in its very bigness: "They count the miles of their seacoast, and the acres under cultivation and the height of the peaks, and revel in large statistics and the bigness generally, and forget how a few men rattle around in a great deal of scenery. They shout their statistics across the Rockies and the desert to New York. The Mississippi Valley is non-existent to the Californian" (249). The idea that the modern media might lead to the emergence of a bicoastal culture in the United States, along a New York–Los Angeles axis, is one of Lindsay's most astute predictions, especially his concern that Hollywood might be out of touch with Middle America.

Lindsay's criticism of California rings true to this day: "The enemy of California says the state is magnificent but thin. . . . He says the citizens of this state lack the richness of an aesthetic and religious tradition" (248). And then Lindsay makes a particularly provocative prediction: "This apparent thinness California has in common with the routine photoplay, which is at times as shallow in its thought as the shadow it throws upon the screen. This newness California has in common with all photoplays. It is thrillingly possible for the state and the art to acquire spiritual tradition and depth together" (248). Today we might make the point this way: Hollywood has about as much depth as a flatscreen TV. Lindsay's doubts about California have been shared by cultural critics ever since. They recurrently charge that a superficial culture in California churns out one superficial movie after another. Yet Lindsay hopes that, sharing a fresh start, the state and the movie industry might together grow into something richer culturally.

Elsewhere Lindsay is less optimistic about having California set the tone for America as a whole: "The moving picture captains of industry, like the California gold finders of 1849, making colossal fortunes in two or three years, have the same glorious irresponsibility and occasional need of the sheriff" (245). In his claim that the nascent movie industry cannot be understood in isolation from the California environment in which it is developing, Lindsay thus finds cause for both optimism and pessimism. By standing for freedom and openness, California epitomizes much that is best in America and is a fitting setting for a young, vibrant, dynamic movie industry. But at the same time, in an equally American way, California poses the threat of lawlessness and a lack of cultural traditions—it is, after all, the last outpost of the Wild West. We cannot fault Lindsay for leaving unresolved the question of whether California's cultural leadership is good or bad for America. We are still struggling with this issue nearly a century later.

What is impressive is that Lindsay was able to formulate this problem as early as 1915. This is exactly the sort of development that usually flies right under the radar of most cultural critics. So what if the movie business relocated to Hollywood? Wasn't it just a matter of year-round sunshine and more light for the cameras? Lindsay was astute enough to spot a cultural tsunami where other people saw only a ripple on the waters. Lindsay teaches an important lesson in cultural prophecy—be on the lookout for seemingly insignificant developments that may have unintended and widespread consequences. In retrospect, we can now see that the shift of the movie industry to Hollywood had as much of a long-term impact on America as the development of the motion picture itself. When it happened, it seemed to be a mere accident of geography and weather, and yet it transformed the soul of America in ways we are still trying to comprehend. The chapter on California in *The Art of the Moving Picture* is Lindsay at his provocative and prophetic best.

SOME MODEST PREDICTIONS

On the basis of what we have learned from studying Lindsay, I will now venture a few modest predictions of my own. The future of American culture will be very different from what we expect it to be or what our best sages currently predict. Some of the things we value in our popular culture today will survive into the future. Familiar motion pictures and television shows will become classics, if they have not done so already, and be treated the way we value the masterpieces of long-established arts, such as literature, painting, and music. These pop culture classics will, for example, be taught in our colleges and universities. By the same token, many things we value in our popular culture will be forgotten, whether rightly or wrongly, and suffer the fate of the vast majority of cultural productions in history—oblivion to all but the most antiquarian of scholars.

Trends that we are barely noticing at the moment will turn out to have had all sorts of unintended consequences and to have transformed American culture in ways we cannot imagine. I wish I could identify where a great subterranean tectonic shift is occurring in American popular culture, but unfortunately I am not up to the task. I will say this much: it is very likely happening in the last place most of us expect it. That generally means that it is not happening in the media realms we have by now become used to and which we therefore think are all-important, namely motion pictures and television. What the history of media teaches us is that new media have a way of sneaking up on us and ambushing us culturally.

It may seem like a massive cop-out to say that the cultural future is simply unpredictable, unimaginable within our current horizons. And yet that is what we observe when we study the actual history of cultural prediction. The contours of the cultural landscape in 2000 would have been virtually unrecognizable to eyes looking forward from 1900. Maybe the first thing we need to do is to acknowledge our limits as cultural prophets, given our past experience with the role. But all this may sound ominous—for me to say that the future is unpredictable may give the impression that only bad things will happen. So let me end on a somewhat optimistic note. I said that the unpredictability of the cultural future reflects the fact that culture is a realm of human freedom and creativity. When we make predictions about the future, we are usually implying that cultural trends are at work that will determine the outcome no matter what creative individuals try to do about it. I do not think this view is true to human nature. We are ultimately not the prisoners of our culture, but its creators.

THE SAME OLD STORY

And let me now take back much of what I have been saying and question whether culture was completely transformed between 1900 and 2000. If we look at the development of the media, as I have been doing, we cannot help being struck by the deep discontinuities. A Late Victorian would be amazed by television and probably at first appalled by it. Confronted by a new medium, we are always struck precisely by its novelty and usually unnerved by it. But what the medium portrays may not be all that new and different. My very late Victorian, surviving into the 1990s, would at first no doubt be shocked by *The Simpsons*. But if he could settle down with the show, he might overcome his initial dismay and begin to see something familiar in it. The fact that it comes in weekly installments, the way it combines humor and sentimentality, the huge cast of quirky and lovable characters, the creation of an entire imaginary community in depth, the topical references and the political satire—after awhile my eminent Victorian might well be saying, "I've seen all this before: it's just like Charles Dickens."

We can get so wrapped up in distinctions among the media that we forget that, by and large, they are all used to do the same thing—to tell stories. And often while the media change, the stories remain the same. Consider the way Dickens stories have kept circulating in movies and on television. Even in the course of media revolutions, somehow much of the old wine manages to survive in the new bottles—because wine often does get better with age. I think that prospect offers cause for hope. I will end with a quotation from a true classic of American popular culture, *Casablanca*: "It's still the same old story, a fight for love and glory." Even "as time goes by." That is the best prediction I can make about our cultural future.

NOTES

1. For my view of *The Simpsons,* see my book *Gilligan Unbound: Pop Culture in the Age of Globalization* (Lanham, MD: Rowman and Littlefield, 2001), 67–109.

2. For an amusing and informative account of this phenomenon, see

James Robert Parish, *Fiasco: A History of Hollywood's Iconic Flops* (Hoboken, NJ: John Wiley, 2006).

3. Edward Bellamy, *Looking Backward* (1888; reprint, New York: Dover, 1996), 55, 67.

4. On this subject, see my essay "Is There Intelligent Life on Television?" *Claremont Review of Books* 13, no. 4 (Fall 2008): 56–59.

5. See, for example, V.F. Perkins, *Film as Film: Understanding and Judging Movies* (New York: Da Capo, 1993), 9–10.

6. Vachel Lindsay, *The Art of the Moving Picture* (1915, 1922; reprint, New York: Liveright, 1970), 202. All future page citations from this (reprint) edition are incorporated into the body of the text.

7. Lindsay probably was unaware that the Chushingura story had been brought to the screen in Japan as early as 1907 and 1908.

8. But Hayakawa did make a remarkable Japanese-themed film in 1919 called *The Dragon Painter,* one of the most visually beautiful films of the silent era. Directed by William Worthington, it was created by the production company Hayakawa formed with Worthington, called Haworth Picture Corporation.

9. This figure is better known today as Tokugawa Ieyasu.

10. See Perkins, *Film as Film,* 10.

11. Given the racist content of *Birth of a Nation,* let me immediately point out, as all film critics do today, that to call the film an "artistic masterpiece" is not to endorse its message but to acknowledge its unquestionable contributions to the development of cinema as an art form.

12. I obtained a copy of the 1915 edition of *The Art of the Moving Picture* (published by Macmillan) and compared it carefully with the 1922 edition (published by Liveright). For the 1922 edition, Lindsay added a new book 1, which consists of twenty-eight pages of new material. He substituted a new "The Point of View" chapter for the original one (each version has seven pages). He added one new sentence at the end of the chapter titled "The Photoplay of Action." And he rewrote the first two pages of the chapter titled "The Intimate Photoplay." Otherwise the 1922 edition appears to repeat the 1915 edition word for word. In sum, the 1922 edition is very close to the 1915 edition.

13. David Shipman, *The Story of Cinema* (New York: St. Martin's, 1982); David Cook, *A History of Narrative Film* (New York: W. W. Norton, 1996).

14. Armed with the name of the director of the film, Laurence "Larry" Trimble, I was at least able to locate *The Battle Hymn of the Republic* in

Ephraim Katz, *The Film Encyclopedia,* 2nd ed. (New York: HarperCollins, 1994), 1362. The film's date is 1911.

15. *Photoplay* was a common synonym for "motion picture" in Lindsay's day, and he uses the term frequently.

16. Hieroglyphics were, in fact, one of the earliest forms of literacy, but Lindsay chooses to view the Egyptian practice as a form of picture writing.

17. For the record, I am aware that the Brooklyn baseball team was not yet called "the Dodgers" at the time Lindsay was writing.

WILL THE POSTFAMILY CULTURE CLAIM AMERICA?

Allan Carlson

Ole and Lena are a mythical Swedish-American couple, probably residing somewhere in Minnesota, notable for their remarkably dysfunctional marriage. One story goes like this:

Ole and Lena have grown old, and one day Ole becomes very sick. Eventually, he is confined to his upstairs bedroom, barely conscious, bedridden, and growing ever weaker. After several weeks of this, the doctor visits and tells Lena: "Vell, Ole's just about a goner. I don't tink he'll survive the night." So Lena, being a practical woman, decides she had better start preparing for all the guests who will be coming to the funeral. She begins to bake, starting with loaves of *limpa*, a Swedish sweet rye bread. The pleasant smell of baking bread is soon wafting through the house. Suddenly, upstairs, Ole's nose twitches and his eyes bolt open. "Limpa," he says. He jerks up into a sitting position, swings his legs around, and climbs out of bed. It's like a miracle! Half walking, half stumbling, he crosses the room, enters the hallway, and starts working his way down the stairs. "Limpa," he says again. He reaches the ground floor, stumbles across the kitchen, and pulls himself into a chair by a table where a loaf of freshly sliced bread sits. He reaches over to take a slice. "Stop that, Ole!" shouts Lena, as she whaps his hand with her spatula. "That *limpa* bread is for *after* the funeral."

We can laugh at Ole and Lena because they are now out of time, characters from an earlier era of Swedish immigration to America. Their "ideal type," we might say, no longer exists. More importantly, their dysfunctional marriage also belongs to another era. Several generations ago, when there *were* real Oles and Lenas, divorce would have been rare in their community. For better and worse, couples remained in unhappy or troubled marriages, perhaps "for the sake of the children," perhaps for other cultural or religious reasons.

Successful jokes usually involve making fun of institutions that are strong and stable. The "marriage joke," a staple of comedians during the 1950s and 1960s, seems to be fading in our time. Symbolically, Rodney Dangerfield, perhaps the last master of the marriage joke, died recently.

It is hard to make fun of an institution that is battered and bruised. Such are marriage and the family in America. Marriage rates are now at record lows in our country. The average age of first marriage is at a record high, for both men and women. The proportion of adults who will never marry is also at a record level. At the same time, the marital fertility rate in America is at a record low. Meanwhile, 40 percent of all births are now outside of wedlock, and this figure is steadily climbing. Cohabitation—"living together without benefit of clergy," as we used to say—grows ever more popular as an alternative to marriage. While the American divorce rate has been fairly stable for a decade or two, it remains at a high level: one of every two marriages still ends in divorce. Finally, "gay rights activists" are clamoring for the right to marry, with some—if uneven—success among the states.

There are those, such as Harvard historian Nancy Cott, who argue that these changes simply represent the inevitable *evolution* of marriage and family, a natural adaptation of a malleable, plastic-like institution to new conditions. Industrialization, modernization, and the quest for equality, Cott concludes, have freed marriage from the shackles of the past, allowing it to evolve into a higher and better form.[1]

There is no doubt that the Industrial Revolution brought new pressures to bear on what I prefer to call the Natural Family. At the most basic level, this process severed the workplace from the home. For all of human history up to that time, the great majority of humans had lived and worked in the same place, be it a small farm or an artisan's shop or a nomad's tent. Under the industrial regime, though, adults were pulled out of their homes to labor in factories or offices. Serious complications arose over matters such as sex or gender roles and the care of children.[2]

However, in most of Europe and North America, families recovered a significant degree of autonomy through "family wage" regimes. Constructed by religious leaders, social reformers, and morally grounded labor unions, family wage systems limited the intrusion of the industrial principle into the family circle. These systems held that the factories could hire only one person per household, normally the husband and father, and that that person should receive a family-sustaining wage. For working-class women, "liberation" came to mean *freedom from having* to work in the factories. This allowed mothers to focus on maintaining autonomous homes and caring for children. In this way, the natural family rooted in marriage and focused on procreation and child-rearing accommodated itself to the new industrial era.[3]

It is also true, though, that "family-wage" regimes of this kind largely vanished during the last three decades of the twentieth century and are now mostly forgotten. Feminist historians, such as Nancy Cott, see this as an important and most welcome step in the evolution of marriage and family. A more accurate interpretation is that the disappearance of these regimes has been a major cause of the deterioration of marriage and family life seen since 1965; while such systems had flaws, nothing compensated for the loss of their strengths. Moreover, rather than being an aspect of social *evolution,* this transformation of private life was the direct result of an ideological project designed to create a *postfamily order.*

This unique ideological effort had both socialist and feminist roots. It was expressed most clearly in Sweden, the ancestral home of Ole and Lena.

Toward a Postfamily Order

The changing status of marriage and family in Sweden over the past one hundred years can be summarized by reference to five transitions:

1. *From* a regime where marriage was an open expression of Christian values with claims of its own *to* a regime that is intentionally secular and designed to protect the interests of the individual;

2. *From* a legal order that granted legal marriage special status *to*

one granting nearly equivalent rights and obligations to non-marital cohabitation;

3. *From* a regime that assumed a breadwinning husband/father and a homemaking wife/mother *to* a regime giving priority to gender equality, universal adult employment, and self-support;

4. *From* a legal order that encouraged marriage as an economic partnership resting on a vital home economy *to* a regime dedicated to what one analyst calls "statisation,"[4] in which the state deliberately *takes over* family functions, *moves* women into state employment and children into state care, *encourages* the *economic independence* of married adults, and crafts universal *dependence* on the welfare state;

5. And *from* a regime that presumed marriage to be exclusively heterosexual and monogamous *to* one that grants nearly equal status, benefits, and obligations to same-sex couples and— soon—to polygamous and other polyamorous arrangements as well.

The foundation of Swedish law remains a vast statute called *Sveriges rikes lag,* enacted in 1734 but now having innumerable amendments.[5] Under the assumption of a "common estate," this measure long codified the subordinate status of women relative to men in matters of income and property. Despite some liberalization in the late nineteenth century, the Swedish husband until 1920 still held the right to control and administer the common estate during marriage. However, reflecting the priority of land and lineage in the old regime, the law excluded from the common estate real property acquired before marriage or by inheritance during marriage. In the then-rare cases of divorce, the marital estate was divided equally, although marital misconduct such as adultery could result in penalties imposed on the offender.[6]

In 1918–1919, the Kingdom of Sweden experienced a bloodless democratic revolution. After mass protests occurred in the streets, the king surrendered virtually all of his power to Parliament. The adoption of universal adult suffrage in 1920 extended the vote to women. And Parliament also adopted that year a new Marriage Code.

This 1920 code built on the idea of the marital home as an economic partnership, with husband and wife equal in rights but different in function. In many respects, it *strengthened the institutional nature of marriage* in the context of an emerging postagrarian, urban-industrial society. Relative to property, the 1920 code adopted the concept of "deferred community." The prescribed marital property system rested on the idea of "separate administration but equal division for one and all." The measure abolished the automatic co-ownership of property during marriage as well as the position of the husband as the dominant administrator. Rather, each spouse could control and administer the property that he or she owned at the time of marriage or acquired later. Notably, the 1920 code also embraced the idea of independent liability; spouses were not held responsible for each other's debts (except for educational expenses for their children and certain direct household expenditures). The code expanded the definition of *marital property* to include property acquired before marriage or by inheritance during marriage. On the dissolution of the marriage through death or divorce or by mutual petition, all marital property was to be divided equally, although the courts retained the power to punish one or the other spouse for marital misconduct. Importantly, the code did lay upon the husband a special responsibility for economic support of his wife and children. Overall, the 1920 code aimed at creating a relatively simple marital property system that minimized disputes and the use of lawyers and encouraged gender specialization within the home. It was ideally suited to a people committed to nearly universal marriage and the avoidance of divorce.[7]

Rival Worldviews

During the early 1930s, a declining marriage rate and a sharply falling fertility rate led to calls for radical changes in the Swedish home. For example, the young socialist intellectual Alva Myrdal generated a furor by calling for "collectivized homes" for Swedish families, where young mothers would join fathers in the full-time labor force, infants and toddlers would be cared for in common nurseries, and meals would be prepared in collectivized kitchens. She actually saw such a facility through to construction. With her husband Gunnar Myrdal, she coauthored in 1934 the book *Kris i befolkningsfrågan* (*Crisis in the Population Question*). They argued that raising the birthrate required radical changes in the nature of marriage and of family. Fathers should be freed from their distinctive breadwinner role and mothers from homemaking. All adults should work, and massive new state welfare benefits funded by a "bachelor tax"—including clothing allowances, day-care subsidies, universal health care, low-interest "marriage loans," and so on—should pay the costs of parenthood. The marital home, under their scheme, would largely cease to be a significant economic unit. Early and universal sex education, freely available contraceptives, and liberalized abortion would ensure that all children in the new order would be *wanted* children. Working through the Royal Population Commission of 1935 and the Swedish Parliament's Women's Work Committee, the Myrdals enjoyed a remarkable influence for the balance of the decade.[8]

After 1940, however, their ideas were in retreat. The onset of World War II and Sweden's perilous position as a "neutral" nation surrounded by Nazi German conquests encouraged a conservative nationalism. Relative to the family, an alternative worldview found in the labor unions—namely that women were to be liberated *from* the labor market rather than liberated to participate *in* it and that men deserved to earn a living "family wage"—gained popularity. Sometimes called "maternalism," this attitude saw Alva Myrdal's egalitarian feminism as part of the problem, not the solution. Capitalists, this socialist claim went, should not be allowed to control the mothers, wives, and daughters of the working class. The labor unions, collectively organized as the LO [*Lans organization*], negotiated in 1938 with employers the historic *Saltsjöbaden* agreement, which crystallized job segregation by gender, reserving the better industrial jobs and the higher wages for the unions' male members.

Some feminist analysts label the consequent 1940–1967 period as "the era of the Swedish housewife." Public policy encouraged the full-time care of small children at home. The marriage rate climbed, while the average age at first marriage fell. Fertility also rose and initiated Sweden's mini–baby boom. As late as 1965, only 3 percent of all Swedish preschool children were in some form of nonparental day care. The "traditional Swedish family," encouraged by the Marriage Code of 1920 and by popular values, seemed solid.[9] Indeed, feminist historians quietly acknowledge that as late as the mid-1960s, there was *no pressure* for change from young Swedish housewives and mothers.[10]

"Red Sweden"

Yet the late 1960s experienced new waves of radicalism. "Eurocommunism" was on the march, while Red Brigades terrorized Italy and West Germany, and France was torn apart by the New Left riots. Meanwhile, Christian values—summarized by one analyst as "responsibility, sacrifice, altruism and the sanctity of long-term commitments [such as marriage]"—began to give way rapidly across Western Europe to a militant "secular individualism" focused on the desires of the self.[11]

Sweden also entered into what a leading feminist historian, Yvonne Hirdman, calls its "Red Years," 1967–1976.[12] At their heart was a massive "gender turn" that radically altered the nature of marriage in Sweden. In 1968 a joint report by the Social Democratic Party and the LO abandoned the "family wage" ideal and concluded, "There are . . . strong reasons for making the two breadwinner family the norm in planning long-term changes within the social insurance system."[13] The next year, Alva Myrdal chaired a major panel, "On Equality," for the Social Democrats. Its report concluded, "In the society of the future, . . . the point of departure must be that every adult is responsible for his/her own support. Benefits previously inherent in married status should be eliminated." The Myrdal Report insisted that true "natural" differences between women and men should pose no barrier to reform. State action should make such innate distinctions insignificant. The report also called for a tax policy based on individual earnings, without preference for *any* "form of cohabitation," Myrdal's new and deflating term for marriage.[14]

Accordingly, in 1969 the Swedish government resolved to fundamentally reform its marriage law. The minister of justice created a Committee of Experts and issued his directives. The committee was to consider whether there was still even a need for marriage law and, if so, how it should be reconfigured. It was to assess the "clearly anachronistic" nature of community property, based as it was on the now-to-be-discarded Christian notion of "one flesh." The committee was also to consider the diminished importance of marital status in Sweden; the new imperative of "personal fulfillment"; the rising demand for divorce; the declining public interest in material property in favor of pensions, annuities, and other claims on the welfare state; and the elevation of gender equality into the cornerstone of Swedish social policy.[15]

In this spirit, Sweden's Parliament approved in 1971 a fundamental reform of the income tax. It abolished the taxation of households through the joint income tax return premised on "income splitting" by married couples. Instead, all persons would henceforth be taxed as individuals, without attention to marital status, dependents, employment, or income of a spouse. This gave Sweden the most "fully individualized taxation system" in the developed world. In the context of high marginal tax rates, this change also greatly benefited the two-income household and penalized the traditional one-income breadwinner family.[16] Analysts of modern Sweden are nearly unanimous in viewing this shift from joint to individual taxation as the most sweeping social change in Sweden over the past forty years, for it "more or less eradicated" the traditional home.[17] As the feminist analyst Annika Baude concludes: "If I were to choose one reform which has . . . done the most to promote equality between the sexes, I would point to the introduction of individual income taxation."[18]

On the basis of the Family Law Reform Committee's work, Parliament approved two years later (1973) a new measure governing marriage and divorce. Access to marriage actually expanded. Most legal impediments to heterosexual marriage disappeared: even half-brothers and half-sisters could marry, as could aunts and nephews, uncles and nieces. Only siblings and persons related by blood in unilinear descent faced prohibition; bigamy and polygamy remained banned. The minimum marriage age for both spouses became eighteen. Premised on the idea of marriage as a voluntary union, it was—in one advocate's words—"only natural that if one of the spouses is dissatisfied, he or she may demand a divorce." In effect, this 1973 law held that the community or the state no longer had significant interests in the preservation of a marriage. "Fault" would no longer be considered, nor would marital misconduct have any bearing on the division of property. This latter change ripped both "adultery" and "fidelity" out of marriage's institutional construct. If both husband and wife agreed to the divorce, it would be immediately granted. If one spouse objected or if there was at least one child under age sixteen in the home, the new law fixed a mandatory reconsideration period of six months. "Separation" no longer had legal status. The measure assumed adult self-support and largely ended the concept of alimony (except in limited cases where "maintenance" payments for a set time might be required).[19]

THE PALME ERA

In 1972 a new Social Democratic prime minister, Olof Palme, came to power. Alva Myrdal joined his cabinet as minister of disarmament and church affairs. Under her open influence, Palme addressed the women of the party that year, declaring an end to the maternalist order. "In this society," he said, "it is only natural for both parents to work. In this society it is evident that man and woman should take the same responsibility for the care of the home and the children." He added, "In this society . . . the care of these future generations is just as naturally the responsibility of us all."[20]

A true revolution began. The party abolished its Women's League, long the bastion of the homemakers. Women would now be "real members" of the party, Palme said, dealing with "common issues" alone. New policies made employment nearly mandatory for all women in their twenties and thirties. Surviving homemakers would pay dearly through heightened marginal taxes on their husbands. Small children now moved massively into day care: 460,000 held places in 1995, compared to only 23,000 three decades earlier.[21]

Yvonne Hirdman correctly gauges the sweep of change here. She notes that women's work in this new Swedish order took on a peculiar quality. In the fields of agriculture and forestry, the number of working women actually declined, while in private industry it grew only modestly. However, in the service sector (heavily governmental in nature), the number of working women rose from 269,000 in 1950 to 819,000 by 1990; in the education and health care sectors (exclusively governmental), the number of working women rose nearly threefold, from 282,000 in 1950 to slightly over 1 million by 1990. In a nation of only 8 million people, these were large changes. In the words of two Israeli sociologists who have studied this change, the Swedish welfare state "channel[ed] women in disproportionate numbers into feminine occupational niches" such as child care, elder care, nursing, and elementary education. Swedish women still did "women's work," but now they did so for the government, rather than for their own families.[22]

Put another way, Sweden successfully socialized "women's work" and the labor of women themselves. The goal of socialism had always been to eliminate the family as a meaningful economic and social unit, so that a husband would no longer be dependent in any way on his wife, nor a wife on her husband, nor young children on parents, nor elderly parents on grown children. All would be equally dependent on the comprehensive welfare state. Pointing specifically to the experience of Alva Myrdal, Hirdman declares triumphantly: "New ideas of gender replaced old-fashioned ideas about the couple. We witness [here] the birth of the androgynous individual (and I speak about the explicit ideal) and the death of the provider and his housewife. We thus witness old ideas popping up, ideas that had been buried for decades—but ideas that very quickly found their advocates and became developed: people, men and women, eager to speak the new tongue of gender."[23]

The Parliament approved the Joint Homes Act in 1987. This new measure governing "relationships similar to marriage" rested on "the principle of neutrality toward family form." As legal analyst Ulla Björnberg explains: "The principle states that individuals are free to develop their personal lives at *their own will*, to *choose a living arrangement* and *ethical norms for their* family life. The role of family law is restricted to providing *solutions* to *practical* problems and to *formulate rules* of a kind that can be accepted by almost all individuals."[24] Still, the Joint Homes Act did not quite equate "cohabitation" with "marriage." Specifically, cohabitators did not gain the equivalence of "marital property rights" in inheritance or a right to claim "maintenance" after separation. Rather, the rules in this measure applied only to the equal splitting of a dwelling and household goods acquired for joint use. However, the measure did affirm that parenthood in consensual unions would involve rights and responsibilities equal to those in marriage. Unmarried fathers must register with the state. Joint custody of children after separation would be the assumption for both cohabiting and married couples. A novel development in the 1987 measure, though, was that it applied to both unmarried heterosexual *and homosexual* couples.[25] I would underscore that this latter innovation came near the end of the de-institutionalizing project, not at its beginning.

In 1995 the Swedish Parliament expanded on this change and approved a law granting same-sex couples the right to form a "registered partnership." This represented a civil contract providing rights and responsibilities nearly identical to those of conventional marriage. The few exceptions involved adoption, joint custody, and artificial insemination. "Registered partners" gained rights to "deferred community property."

In 2000 the government severed its official ties to the Lutheran Church of Sweden, bringing a symbolic end to "Christian Sweden"— although the country had been effectively de-Christianized some decades earlier. The same year, the Swedish government extended the "registered partnership" option to foreign nationals who had resided in Sweden for at least two years. In 2002 gay and lesbian couples gained the right to adopt children (although during the first year of this law's operation, none did so). Recent Swedish Court decisions have also given legal recognition to polygamous marriages among immigrants from Muslim countries. An association of informal Swedish polygamists predicts full recognition of plural marriages and other polyamorous relations in their land, in the near future.[26]

In America?

Has this same postfamily culture, built on socialist and feminist assumptions, made any progress in America? Have Americans also learned how to speak "the new tongue of gender" and accommodated themselves to the vast expansion of government that it seems to require? They have, although in more convoluted and less obvious ways. The Swedes, at least, debated these issues more or less in the open. American debates have *rarely* been as clear and focused. All the same, key changes have included these:

- *In July 1964,* the U.S. House of Representatives voted to add the word "sex" to Title VII of the proposed Civil Rights Act, the section prohibiting discrimination in employment. The amendment was actually offered by a curious coalition of Dixiecrat segregationists and Republican feminists. The former hoped to use this amendment to kill the whole measure; the latter group saw an opportunity to tear down the American family wage regime. A few profamily voices warned of dire consequences, yet this curious coalition carried the day.[27] Starting in 1969, the Equal Employment Opportunity Commission moved aggressively—and successfully—to eliminate the American family wage. Indeed, between 1970 and 1990, the real wages of men fell by 20 percent, pushing more women into the labor market, simply to make ends meet.[28]

- *Also in 1969,* the U.S. Congress approved a major Tax Reform bill. House Ways and Means Committee Chairman Wilbur Mills, responding to criticism from singles that the tax code favored marriage, successfully ended the practice of "income splitting." The tax burden carried by married couples rose, and the "marriage tax penalty"—which still haunts us today—emerged.[29]

- *In 1973,* the United States came within a hair's breadth of creating a massive federal "child development" entitlement. Fortunately, President Richard Nixon vetoed the measure. In a statement reportedly drafted by his aide Patrick J. Buchanan, Nixon said the bill would have committed "the vast moral authority of the federal government to the side of communal approaches to child rearing as against the child-centered approach." Alas, Congress turned around and quickly approved several other measures providing day-care grants to the poor and child-care tax credits for the middle and upper classes.[30]

- The broad results in America have also been in the same direction as Sweden. It is true that our welfare state still remains somewhat limited; our voluntary religious and charitable sectors are still relatively vital; and the accelerated flow of American women into the labor force has been more complex and pluralistic than in Sweden. All the same, government transfer payments to individuals—a reliable measure of welfare state activity—have grown from $263 billion in 1980 to $1.548 *trillion* in 2006; even after taking inflation into account, the number has nearly tripled. Also, much as it occurred in Sweden, the great influx of women into the workforce has been channeled heavily into the governmental sector.[31] And three out of every four American preschool children are also now in nonparental day care, all federally subsidized.

In short, tasks that were formerly performed by families in their own homes—primary health care; infant, toddler, and after-school care; maternal nursing; and so on—have been substantially turned over to the state or to state-funded entities: "public patriarchy," some feminist theorists label it. Higher taxes, which have fallen with particular force on the remaining one-income homes with three or more children, have helped pay the cost. Achieved incrementally and with few open ideological clashes, this might be called the Swedish "postfamily" model via the American plan.

A series of federal court decisions since 1965 reinforced the process. In *Griswold v. Connecticut,* the U.S. Supreme Court overturned a state law prohibiting the possession and use of contraceptives. While cleverly appealing to the "sacred precincts of the bedroom" and to the nearly "sacred" nature of marriage, the Court here used a new "right to privacy" to sever the presumptive linkage of marriage to procreation.[32] Seven years later, the Court struck down a ban on the use of contraceptives by the unmarried, as well, now arguing that "the marital couple is not an independent entity with a mind and heart of its own, but an association of two individuals each with a separate intellectual and emotional make up." This decision in *Eisenstadt v. Baird* not only dismissed talk about the sacred nature of marriage; by equating unmarried and married couples, it also shattered the presumptive licit monopoly of the married state over sexual activity.[33]

Other Court decisions weakening the legal standing of the family followed. In 1976 the Supreme Court used the right of privacy to strip the father of an unborn child—whether married or not—of any right to affect a mother's decision to have an abortion.[34] A year later, the Court also stripped parents and state governments of any controls over the possession and use of contraceptives by minor children. Here again, "privacy" trumped family autonomy; the Court ruled, "It is clear that among the decisions that an individual may make without justified interference are personal" ones, including the use of birth control.[35] A 1971 decision by the Supreme Court struck down a state law that placed financial requirements on indigent persons seeking divorce, turning a "freedom to marry" into a "freedom to divorce without cost."[36] In the celebrated case of *Marvin v. Marvin,* the California Supreme Court ruled that cohabitating couples could claim some of the legal financial obligations formerly attached only to marriage. In effect, the distinction between marriage and nonmarriage diminished again.

The overall effects of these and related decisions was to push America toward the same deconstruction of marriage and the institutional family as seen in Sweden. What began as an institution focused on procreation, fidelity, permanence, and social order had become instead a highly personalized extension of the welfare state.

All the same, there are important pockets of resistance, and all of them are growing. Most dramatically, homeschool families have mobilized to defend the integrity of their home economies by focusing on the most important of family responsibilities: education. Emerging in the face of state hostility, they have won legal recognition across the country and are producing a disproportionate number of the nation's morally grounded and creative young adults. They are a special embarrassment to public schools, which have been operating on a socialist industrial model for over a century, with ever more discouraging results.[37]

Some American religious groups have done a solid job in building new affirmations of the natural family. Under the leadership of figures such as Paige Patterson and Albert J. Mohler, for example, the Southern Baptist Convention is developing a powerful new pro-family apologetic.[38] The Latter-day Saints, or Mormons, provide an important contemporary example of how—in the face of cultural turmoil—a denomination can foster and maintain its own "culture of marriage," with measurable positive results.[39]

I also find reason for optimism in the growing number of home businesses in America. In 2005 there were 21.5 million sole proprietorships in America, an increase of 50 percent since 1990. Taking advantage of new technologies such as the home computer and the economic democracy of the Internet, they are powering a new age of family entrepreneurship. More importantly from a world-historic perspective, they are beginning to heal the great breach between work and home, a divide exploited by the advocates of the postfamily order.

Ronald Reagan understood what was at stake. He noted in 1984 that throughout American history Americans had "relied on the family as the principal institution for transmitting values."[40] From 1986 to the end of his presidency, Reagan gave mounting attention to strengthening the nation's family system. "The family provides children with a haven of love and concern," he told the Student Congress on Evangelism. "For parents, it provides a sense of purpose and meaning in life. When the family is strong, the nation is strong. When the family is weak, the Nation itself is weak."[41] He raised up the example of the Hispanic *casa,* or home, for all Americans, calling it "the almost mystical center of daily life, where grandparents and parents and children and grandchildren all come together in the *familia.*"[42] And, in a speech given in Chicago in 1988, he said: "The family is the bedrock of our nation, but it is also the engine that gives our country life. . . . It's for our families that we work and labor, so that we can join around the dinner table, bring our children up the right way, care for our parents, and reach out to those less fortunate. It is the power of the family that holds the Nation together, that gives America her conscience, and that serves as the cradle of our nation's soul."[43]

So true. And in their better moments, even Ole and Lena would agree.

Notes

1. Nancy F. Cott, *Public Vows: A History of Marriage and the Nation* (Cambridge, MA: Harvard Univ. Press, 2001).

2. See Karl Polanyi, *The Great Transformation* (New York: Farrar and Rinehart, 1944), 39.

3. Allan Carlson, *Third Ways: How Bulgarian Greens, Swedish Housewives, and Beer-Swilling Englishmen Created Family-Centered Economies—And Why They Disappeared* (Wilmington, DE: ISI Books, 2007), 35–60.

4. The term *statisation* is used in D. Bradley, "Marriage, Family, Property and Inheritance in Swedish Law," *International and Comparative Law Quarterly* 39 (April 1990): 380.

5. Michael Bogdan and Eva Ryrstedt, "Marriage in Swedish Family Law and Swedish Conflicts of Law," *Family Law Quarterly* 29 (Fall 1995): 675–76.

6. See Bradley, "Marriage, Family, Property and Inheritance in Swedish Law," 373–74.

7. Ibid., 373–78.

8. Alva Myrdal and Gunnar Myrdal, *Kris i befolkningsfrågan* (Stockholm: Bonniers, 1934); and, more broadly, Allan Carlson, *The Swedish Experiment in Family Politics: The Myrdals and the Interwar Population Crisis* (New Brunswick, NJ: Transaction, 1990), chaps. 3–5.

9. Yvonne Hirdman, "The Importance of Gender in the Swedish Labor Movement; or, A Swedish Dilemma," 3–5, a paper prepared for the Swedish National Institute of Working Life, 2002; Ann-Katrin Hatje, *Befolkningsfrågan och välfärden: Debatten om familjepolitik och nativitetsökning under 1930-och 1940-talen* (Stockholm: Allmänna förlaget, 1974).

10. Dorothy McBride Stetson and Amy Maxur, eds., *Comparative State Feminisms* (Thousand Oaks, CA: Sage, 1995), 241.

11. Ron Lesthaeghe, "A Century of Demographic and Cultural Change in Western Europe: An Exploration of Underlying Dimensions," *Population and Development Review* 9 (1983): 429.

12. Hirdman, "The Importance of Gender in the Swedish Labor Movement."

13. Jane Lewis and Gertrude Åström, "Equality, Difference, and State Welfare: Labor Market and Family Politics in Sweden," *Feminist Studies* 18 (Spring 1992): 67.

14. Alva Myrdal et al., *Toward Equality: The Alva Myrdal Report to the Swedish Social Democratic Party* (1969; reprint, Stockholm: Prisma, 1972), 17, 38, 64, 82–84, quotation on 82.

15. Fariborz Nozari, "The 1987 Swedish Family Law Reform," *International Journal of Legal Information* 17 (1989): 219–20; Bradley, "Marriage, Family, Property and Inheritance in Swedish Law," 378–81.

16. Irene Dingledey, "International Comparison of Tax Systems and Their Impact on the Work-Family Balancing," at www.latge.de/ak tuellveroeff/am/dinge100b.pdf, accessed November 5, 2003.

17. Anne Lise Ellingsaeter, "Dual Breadwinner Societies: Provider Models in the Scandinavian Welfare States," *Acta Sociologica* 41, no. 1

(1998): 66; Sven Steinmo, "Social Democracy vs. Socialism: Goal Adaptation in Social Democratic Sweden," *Politics and Society* 16 (December 1988): 430; Maud L. Edwards, "Toward a Third Way: Women's Politics and Welfare Policies in Sweden," *Social Research* 58 (Fall 1991): 681–82.

18. Annika Baude, "Public Policy and Changing Family Patterns in Sweden, 1930–1977," in *Sex Roles and Social Policy: A Complex Social Equation,* ed. Jean Lipman-Blumen and Jessie Bernard (Beverly Hills, CA: Sage, 1979), 171.

19. Bogdan and Ryrstedt, "Marriage in Swedish Family Law," 678–79; Nozari, "The 1987 Swedish Family Law Reform," 220–23.

20. *SAP Congress Minutes, 1972,* 759, quoted in Hirdman, "The Importance of Gender in the Swedish Labor Movement," 6.

21. Anita Myberg, "From Foster Mothers to Child Care Center: A History of Working Mothers and Child Care in Sweden," *Feminist Economics* 6, no. 1 (2000): 15–16.

22. Hadas Mandel and Moshe Semgonov, "A Welfare State Paradox: State Interventions and Women's Employment Opportunities in 22 Countries," *American Journal of Sociology* 111 (May 2006): 1913, 1916.

23. Hirdman, "The Importance of Gender in the Swedish Labor Movement," 10.

24. Ulla Björnberg, "Cohabitation and Marriage in Sweden—Does Family Form Matter?" *International Journal of Law, Policy, and the Family* 15 (2001): 352–53, emphasis added.

25. Ibid., 350–62.

26. See Karl-Göran Bottwyk, "Polygamy in Sweden," at www.nccg.org/fecpp/sweden.html, accessed May 16, 2005.

27. See Paul Adam Blanchard, "Insert the Word 'Sex'—How Segregationists Handed Feminists a 1964 'Civil Rights' Victory against the Family," *Family in America* 12 (March 1998): 1–12.

28. Donald Allen Robinson, "Two Movements in Pursuit of Equal Employment Opportunity," *Signs* 4, no. 3 (1979): 42.

29. See Allan Carlson, *Fractured Generations: Crafting a Family Policy for Twenty-first Century America* (New Brunswick, NJ: Transaction, 2005), 96.

30. Ibid., 48.

31. See Francis Fox Piven, "Ideology and the State: Women, Power, and the Welfare State," in *Women, the State, and Welfare,* ed. Linda Gordon (Madison: Univ. of Wisconsin Press, 1990), 251–64.

32. Griswold v. Connecticut, 381 U.S. 486 (1965).

33. Eisenstadt v. Baird, 495 U.S. 438, 453 (1972).

34. Planned Parenthood of Missouri v. Danforth, 428 U.S. 52, 69 (1976).

35. Carey v. Population Services International, 431 U.S. 679 (1977).

36. Boddie v. Connecticut, 401 U.S. 371 (1971). See also Carl Anderson, "The Supreme Court and the Economics of the Family," *Family in America* 1 (October 1987): 3.

37. See Mitchell Stevens, *The Kingdom of Children: Culture and Controversy in the Homeschooling Movement* (Princeton, NJ: Princeton Univ. Press, 2001).

38. See the 1998 SBC Resolution on the Family Foundation, www.bsc.org/synod/resolutions/062_18.html.

39. See The First Presidency and Council of the Twelve Apostles of the Church of Jesus Christ of Latter-day Saints, "The Family: A Proclamation to the World," September 23, 1995, at http://lds.org/library/display/0,4945,161–1-11–1,00.html, accessed February 20, 2010.

40. Ronald Reagan, "Remarks at a Presentation Ceremony for the 1983 Young American Medals for Bravery, August 28, 1984," in *Public Papers of the Presidents: Ronald Reagan, 1984* (Washington, DC: Government Printing Office, 1985), 1202.

41. Reagan, "Remarks to the Student Congress on Evangelism, July 28, 1988," in *Public Papers of the Presidents of the United States, Ronald Reagan: 1981–1988–89* (Washington, DC: Government Printing Office, 1982–1991), 992.

42. Reagan, "Remarks on Signing the National Hispanic Heritage Week Proclamation, September 13, 1988," in *Papers, Reagan: 1988–89*, 1158–59.

43. Reagan, "Remarks at a Luncheon with Community Leaders in Chicago, Illinois, September 30, 1988," in *Papers, Reagan: 1988–89*, 1252.

THE CRITIC AND CULTURE

Jean Bethke Elshtain

Everybody's a critic. It seems to be a natural right among Americans to gripe about pretty much everything, but government above all. How many times have you heard the plaint "They are all a bunch of crooks," that politics is an innately dirty game. Trust in politicians and the political process is at a nadir among us. In addition, for many decades, cultural elites anointed themselves the designated critics of the culture. Much of their criticism consisted of treating with contempt popular or low culture, by contrast to the high culture of which they claimed they were the keepers. Today, elite criticism finds in the outpourings of ordinary citizens about the state of our union nothing but ignorant fanaticism. And so it goes. We hear a good bit of shouting, but it is difficult to penetrate, hard to get our bearings. As a result, in order to counter elite critique, some suggest that criticizing the country in severe terms is tantamount to a lack of patriotism. The predictable response is that the only worthy patriot is the critic.

CULTURAL CRITICISM AND THE LOVE OF COUNTRY

It is not my intent to make my way through all this noise. Instead, I want to start at "another place," as we say. When we think about the Hebrew prophets of old, we are reminded that they were part of, and loved, the people, the Israelites, they were criticizing. They did not see themselves as above it all or on the outside. Reminding myself of this, I recalled a very wise comment made several years ago in a speech by Cardinal Francis George of the great city of Chicago. He stated, "You cannot criticize effectively what you do not love." He had in mind criticism of the church that, from all too many quarters, comes from a stance of bitter animus.

One can find similar animus at work in too many criticisms of contemporary America. It is the flip side of the old notion of American exceptionalism. You have some idea of what that entailed—the claim that America was an exceptional nation that was anointed in a historic sense to carry on a particular mission in the world, one that lifted up at all times and carried forward the message of freedom.

The position of American exceptionalism gets a very bad press nowadays, but there were several versions of it. One lent itself to aggressive nationalism; another, to robust patriotism—America was indeed exceptional in a number of ways; that was simply a fact—but that did not demand that we treat the loves others had for their particular countries lightly. Instead, we recognized that love and worked with it, so to speak.

Surely Abraham Lincoln's idea, put forward in the agony of his country at the time, that America is "the last best hope on earth," is an expression of the gentler form of American exceptionalism. Still, there are among us critics who make no distinction whatsoever between the belligerent and the more pacific versions of American exceptionalism, critics who condemn it without restraint. But they do so in a manner that is itself a species of a noxious form of American exceptionalism, namely, representing America as the leading exemplar of injustice, racism, imperialism, classism, capitalism run amok, venal globalism—you name it, if it is bad, we embody it.

Put forward as criticism, this quickly becomes a type of conspiracy theory: if anything bad is happening somewhere, America's bloody hands are bound to be involved. In response to this sort of virulent outburst, the defender of America may well go overboard in another direction and exonerate us altogether of historic sins, crimes, and misdemeanors, offering up a too rosy view about us and everything we have done.

Thus we find a great deal of back-and-forth that is labeled criticism but takes us nowhere; it is by now so much background static that does not assist the ordinary citizen in thinking about how we might go about loving our country and criticizing it at the same time. Those who do not love their country as American citizens will be entirely unmoved by the argument I will set forth. So be it. You can't win 'em all, as they say.

NIEBUHR'S CULTURAL CATEGORIES

Let me step back and think about a framework set forth many years ago now by Reinhold Niebuhr's less famous brother, H. Richard Niebuhr, himself a distinguished theologian. In an "oldie but goodie" called *Christ and Culture,* Niebuhr identified five different positions taken by Christians historically in their relationship to the wider cultural surround in which they found themselves. These were Christ against culture; the Christ of culture; Christ above culture; Christ and culture in paradox; and Christ as the transformer of culture.[1] Can we take our bearings as we think about criticism more generally, whether it comes from a stance of Christian belief or not, from Niebuhr's categories? I think we can.

Is the critic against or above her or his own society? Does the critic seek to transform the society from within? Is there a paradoxical relationship between critic and culture? How do we sort this out, and why is it important?

Niebuhr was insistent that the possibilities he proffered were not airtight categories—they blended into one another at many points. Thus, Christ against culture and Christ as transformer of culture need not be seen as opposites but can be treated as part and parcel of an overall critical stance. But the "against" part cannot be one that is stand-alone, involving brittle condemnation from a haughty presumed moral superiority.

Niebuhr's categories help us to take our bearings conceptually because they identify strong tendencies. For example: as stand-alone categories, Christ against culture and Christ as transformer of culture may turn into brittle condemnation and a stance of moral superiority. Transformation may degenerate into naive idealism, even utopianism, a stance concerning which anti-Nazi German theologian Dietrich Bonhoeffer reserved some of his most severe words. Thus, when I hear contemporary radical critics who seemingly loathe the America they criticize, I am reminded of Bonhoeffer's harsh assessment of "the radical."

The radical begrudges God his creation, Bonhoeffer insists, for the radical seeks a self-sovereignty incompatible with recognition of our indebtedness to others in the past as well as in the present. The radical is all ultimacy, prepared to sacrifice the penultimate, the here and now, for some eschatological goal. That is to say, all "good" is located at some future point. All we have now is bad, loathsome. We must rid ourselves of this present through any and all possible means. If that demands trampling on people's lives, controlling them from above, ignoring their cries for relief and understanding, well, so be it. The radical knows better somehow.[2]

This is not a stance the Christian can embrace, argues Bonhoeffer, for creation is good. That means there must be good to embrace in the present. There are, after all, blessings all around us, even in the most dire circumstances—and Bonhoeffer's were dire beyond anything we can imagine, although, if you believe some of our most belligerent critics, they are in danger (or were during the Bush administrations) of a Gestapo-like entity that may burst through the door and haul them off for their political advocacy any moment. I do not exaggerate.

A few years ago when I attended a conference in Berlin, there were prominent American and German intellectuals who claimed that Guantanamo Bay had been set up to become a prison camp where American citizens critical of the Bush administration would be sent. This was so preposterous one didn't know what to say—other than, "That is preposterous." But doing so, in turn, engendered knowing looks all around that you were either a suspicious sympathizer of the Bush administration or you had your head in the sand and did not know what was coming down the pike! Mind you, this was a view shared by a few who "seconded the motion," so to speak, but no one was prepared to openly challenge such nonsense other than myself and one other person.

Now, of course, there is an exact mirror image of the radical negation stance to be found in what might be called radical affirmation. In Niebuhr's categorization, this would call on the "Christ with culture" side. I refer here to those who equate all that is good with American culture; who brook no criticism; who grow heated and defensive when you note our historic shortcomings and our present hubris, on display from time to time. As the negative radicals find you in league with the "enemy" if you do not agree with them 100 percent, so the totalistic defender of all things American, who equates America with a religious stance, sees you as a dangerous and perhaps unpatriotic American if you criticize your country. You get lumped in with the radical negators.

Neither of these stances embodies authentic cultural critique: one critic overdoes it to the point of loathing her own country and finding nothing good in it; the other rejects and abandons her birthright as a thinking being and a citizen by endorsing as "good" all that is going on. Surely this cannot be, either—certainly not if you are a Christian and hold that human beings are fallen creatures. Christians were enjoined both to love the world and to be "against" the world, contra mundum. Similarly, citizens should both love their country— if that country is at least a minimally decent place, and America meets that standard and goes far beyond it—and understand when and where their country must be held to account, even chastised. They do this because they love the country and want it to rise closer to that "blessed community" of which Martin Luther King, one of our civic prophets, spoke.[3]

THE CONNECTED CRITIC

Let me offer an example of what political theorist Michael Walzer calls "the connected critic," the person who speaks from a stance of deep immersion in that which he criticizes.[4] Who does not exist in some lofty world apart. Who does not send down thundering lightning bolts of condemnation on any and all who disagree with him. Here there are many examples to choose from. Mine will be Frederick Douglass, the great abolitionist, from a speech he delivered in Rochester, New York, on July 4, 1862.

Much of the speech is pointed, even bitter. You cannot drag a man in fetters, enchained, before the altar of liberty and expect him to celebrate on a day that mocks his condition, Douglass cries, going on to offer a blistering comparison of the condition of the slave when measured against the Declaration of Independence and the Preamble to the Constitution. But then he goes on to say: Mind you, I am not condemning the principles, the great principles, in those documents. I share them. The slave aspires to them. We want to be part of the country, not apart from it. We, too, want to be free citizens.[5]

So you see the dynamic here. In Niebuhr's schema, it would be Christ with and against culture. The Christian criticizes and extols. So, I submit, does the critical patriot, whether he is a believer or not. The aim of criticism is transformation. The critic in America is so fortunate, because our civic aims can always be measured against our great founding documents. We do not have to invent anew every day some principles to guide us, a task that is impossible in any case. So the basic questions for the critics will be measured against our ideals of ordered liberty, freedom consistent with a common good, human dignity, and America as the "last best hope" that alerts us to our responsibilities in the world at large.

If the critic functions entirely outside this framework, her criticism will, at best, be irrelevant. We do not need to import full-blown ideologies from Marxism or hard-core libertarianism or some other stance to serve as a basis for criticism—not if we are deeply connected to the American polity and acknowledge our love for and indebtedness to America.

I have thought about that indebtedness a lot recently, perhaps because as one grows older one reflects in greater detail on one's past. My immigrant grandparents of beloved memory, on my mother's side of the family, came here as children, impoverished "Volga Germans." They did stoop labor in the sugar beet fields of northern Colorado, living at first in sod huts, where they found themselves covered with layers of dirt as they awakened every morning. They were out there every day with the hot noontime sun beating down—and that can really get brutal in Colorado—working until dusk, starting again at dawn. Eventually, once my grandparents had married, they slowly acquired a bit of land, which expanded to a bit more.

But the dawn-to-dusk work didn't lighten very much at all. That, indeed, is the image with which I associate them: always working hard, loving their families, and insisting that their children—including my mother, who left school after the eighth grade to work on the farm—gain an uninterrupted education for some of their own children. How quickly things went from that economic hardship and daily, relentless work to grandchildren and great-grandchildren who are doctors, lawyers, professors; as civic benefactors of all kinds, they are like their grandparents and great-grandparents before them, deeding a legacy of decency, hard work, love of faith, love of family, love of country.

How could I possibly condemn outright a country that made all this possible for me? The element of loathing and resentment in so much contemporary criticism, coming from people who are living lives America made possible, is beyond me. So I remain a connected critic, a critical patriot, one who understands what an astonishing proposition America is and how it must never be an object of idolatry but neither should be an object of scorn.

With that, let me turn to an item that speaks to and from the "contra mundum" side of the ledger: Christ against culture. One should never wax romantic about one's country. We can and should affirm the works of human beings and the creative spark we bring to our activities. But contra mundum is also part and parcel of the picture, so long as it does not harden into an ideological stance of some sort. We do face troubles in our culture, many of them touching on the most vulnerable among us, namely, our children. Several years ago an article in the *New York Times* caught my attention.[6] The article informed us of the startling and alarming fact that the use of antipsychotics by young people in the United States had risen fivefold in a single decade. Unless American children are suddenly being overtaken by psychoses, this datum calls for sober analysis and criticism. What does this medicalization of childhood portend? How does one explain it? What should we do about it?

The culture boosters will appear before us decked out in sunny hues and tell us that the feeding of antipsychotic drugs to America's children arises from ever more vigilant care and attunement to the needs of the young. But we cannot take that at face value. Medicine does not exist in a cordon sanitaire, free from the influences of economic and cultural forces. What are the problems being treated? "Aggression" and "mood swings," we are told, in addition to that old standby "attention deficit disorder."

Such a basic piece of cultural information matters to the believer. To embrace the Christ who is both with and against culture, hence the affirmer and critic and transformer of culture, is to be particularly attuned to a culture's children. It is also to become aware of their complexity and diversity—not the bean-counting variety of diversity that currently obtains but, rather, the diverse gifts and qualities that distinguish one child from another, even in the same family. How do we nourish each child's particular qualities and gifts?

The Critic's Challenge

That, in turn, brings us to the general cultural milieu, one in which the norm is both parents working outside the home, coming home exhausted. This milieu values, drives, and measures success through monetary reward. It glamorizes celebrity and ignores the hard work people do every day to raise children and to sustain neighborhoods; to make life less brutal and more kind. Ours is a milieu of pervasive family fragmentation if not outright breakdown, to which many children respond with anger. In this environment, every personal question gets medicalized and psychologized, as do many public questions: new drugs are touted via lavish marketing stratagems.

Christians bringing their reflections on these cultural facts begin with the gifts and integrity of the bodies and beings of children. They go on to consider the gift of time and how precious it is. They remind themselves of the concreteness of the Christian message: do unto others here and now, not in the distant future, not in some abstract way. This, in turn, invites critical reflection on whether we are rushing to diagnose children as "troubled" or "hyperactive" in part because parents no longer spend concentrated time with their children and prefer for them to be pacified when they are with them. Such reflection suggests that radical and uncontrolled experimentation on America's children by way of powerful drugs, many with deleterious side effects and absent knowledge of long-range effects, is undertaken as much for the convenience of adults as it is for the benefit of children.

We recall moments from the past when children—and adults—were quickly labeled "incorrigible," then institutionalized and forgotten. Now we think we are humane in rushing to medicalize, often against the advice of cautious voices within the medical community as to the alleged benefits and many known dangers of massive drug use. One doctor cited in the article spoke of children who had been put on "three or four different drugs," each one of which created new side effects. The doctor went on to ask, "How do you even know who the kid is anymore?"

That is a frightening sentence: how do you even know who this child is? We should be alarmed by a social milieu within which the pacification of children, rather than care and attention to each child in his or her particularity, becomes a social norm. Minimally, we must take a hard look at how children are faring in our society. That, in turn, can spur transformation as we take up "the politics of time." Good, old-fashioned time is what so many children need. How can a society that pretends to be child-centered justify culturally approved neglect? It goes without saying that neglect comes in many forms: thousands of privileged children are neglected in the way I am noting here.

A second item, this one from *Time Out New York,* grabbed my attention back then—in 2006, it was—under the heading "Get Naked," a regular feature in which the magazine's "sexpert" explores the "ins and outs of love and lust." In this issue the "sexpert" congratulated a mother who had written extolling the joys of masturbation discovered by her precocious seven-year-old daughter, who then proceeded to want to know all there was to know about the penis. The mother had decided to enlighten her seven-year-old with photographs by Robert Mapplethorpe, whose explicit images of male genitalia in different postures of sex acts between males stirred up a controversy a few years ago.

Even the "sexpert" caviled at this. Perhaps that went a bit too far, he suggested, for there are other ways to educate about the penis. He closed by extolling the mother's "shame-free attempts to give [her] daughter the information she [needed] to become a well-adjusted, self-empowered individual." Of course, the mom should be alert to all the meanies out there who might try to fill her daughter's brain with "body-detesting nonsense," presumably along the lines of: "When you're a bit older we'll discuss these things," or, "You know that just isn't appropriate. Let's think of something else to do," or "Respecting your body means to take care of it and not just to use it for any purpose."

"Well-adjusted, self-empowered"—the mantra of our time. And well-adjusted means no worries, no shame. Everything is to be uncovered, everything displayed. "Self-empowered" means one can do any-thing and everything that gives one pleasure, although whether that will bring joy is quite another matter. Where does one start with this pack of nonsense and untruths? The Christian repairs to the story of Creation and Fall. We cannot escape human shortcoming and sin. To pretend that stark nakedness, unveiling everything, is the "innocent" ideal is to pretend we are back in the Garden and that human beings have no history. It is to pretend that the categories of good and evil no longer apply; one is truly in a world beyond good and evil. We have seen what such a world looks like, a world fabricated by those who believed they were supermen beyond normative constraint, and it is a cruel, systematically horrific world.

We should not be fooled. Cultural mavens preaching the gospel of the "well-adjusted" purport to embrace what is "natural" when, in fact, their ministrations disrupt the natural, or so Dietrich Bonhoef-fer argues, because they treat life in a manner that misuses freedom. The Christian tradition offers numerous ways to articulate those limits, but discussion of them is beyond the scope of an immodest essay. Yet articulate them we must, for those who embrace a shame-free life (not shameless, one notices) that assaults the integrity of our bodily-ness, in this case exploiting a seven-year-old child to promote a cultural agenda not the child's own, using the child's body to score a point in favor of destroying shame and abrogating limits.

A seven-year-old should be discovering the joys of friendship and learning, finding how to make her way in the world, and imagining and preparing for a future. Instead, and by the mother's own account, the child masturbated at will, was self-obsessed, and demanded more information on "private parts," private no more in the shame-free cul-ture. The Christian can remind the culture that crossing the barrier of shame is a very dangerous thing and must be considered carefully. Minimally, eradicating shame in the name of being "well-adjusted" must be questioned and challenged at every point. The world is a vast laboratory for our consideration. There is much to embrace. But there is also a good deal to condemn, yes, condemn, even as Christ condemned the money changers in the temple. As Bonhoeffer wrote, such condemnation must flow from the Christian not as a "despiser of men," but as one who loves and cares for the world.

A Christian counterculture cannot simply be "counter" if it is to enact projects for the common good. People quite reasonably resist the ministrations of those whose proclamations are all negation. Confronted with such jeremiads, we tend to focus on what's eating such people, why their lives are all bitterness and rue, rather than on what may be vital and true about the message. If, instead, one criticizes in a manner that displays one's love and concern for the culture and the country of which one is a part, others are more apt to pay attention, for one approaches them from a stance of respect.

POLITICS, CULTURE, AND THE CHURCH

In many ways, this would be a good place to stop. But there is a feature or dimension to this question that a cultural critic, especially one who aspires to or acquires the designation "public intellectual," can and must take into account. That is the site wherein cultural and political understanding and criticism of the sort I endorse may be nurtured. About a decade and a half ago, enormous concern was expressed in many quarters about the state of American civil society—that vitally important world of associations limned so perceptively by Alexis de Tocqueville a century and a half ago. For Tocqueville, this world was not officially governmental, but it was intrinsically civic, and it defined the fledgling American republic in vital ways. He was amazed by the alacrity with which Americans rushed to form associations and groups, to take up exigent issues and to turn them into civic concerns. Here he observed women playing a vital role. The civil-society realm creates and maintains the mores, the world of ideas, norms, and convictions that defines the sort of people we are and the sort of polity we inhabit.

Fast-forward from Tocqueville to the year 1995: political scientists told us that there were millions of fewer volunteers; that civic education had more or less collapsed; that people had turned away from things "civic" in massive numbers. This meant, as well, that we had turned our backs on the possibility of commonalities—essential to any democratic project—and hunkered down defensively in "identity groups," insisting that in this alone could one's interests be realized. Of course, this picture required nuance and interpretation, but let's accept it as accurate, at least in the tendencies it named. If the data was at all reliable, democratic citizens faced a thinning out of the concept of the "civic."

Part of the problem, according to scholars, was that many sites of civic formation and deliberation had simply disappeared: the corner grocery stores, the union shops, the local post offices, the neighborhood eateries, even our churches. Even the churches? This was interesting, for America remains more churched than any other Western democracy. Churches have always been a central feature of our civil society, given our fructifying combination of a secular government with a civil society in which religion and politics interact—and always have. Facing this civic gap, some proposed a new notion of "deliberative democracy" in which experts facilitated civic discussions. But these arguments were often so complex and abstract that there was very little the ordinary citizen could draw upon. Besides, in our crazily busy lives, who had the time to master some abstract vocabulary in order to participate in a discourse put forward by social scientists?

So ordinary folks continued to take their bearings elsewhere. And here there should, presumably, be a Christian difference, a "value added," as our economist friends would put it. Indeed this proved to be the case in one important sense. All the data was solid: those who attended church regularly were more likely to put their shoulders to the wheels in local, community affairs—in civic life, mostly but not exclusively of the social ministry sort. In fact, America's churchgoers were carrying the civic burden for the rest of us. But were there distinctive marks of this Christian activity? On display, certainly, was Christian caring—caritas—in the vast array of "social ministries" so central to contemporary Christian bodies. So, yes, for nitty-gritty on-the-ground effort, you were more likely to find believers in the ranks than unbelievers.

If you are interested in critical citizenship, however, in the connected-critic possibility I noted earlier, the food and blood drives and suicide hotlines do not in themselves suffice. Should not the churches also be sites for teaching that has direct implications for civic life, for how we think about what kind of people we are or could become? One challenge Christians face is how to speak when they go public. That question is not my primary focus. What I have in mind is what churches might offer by way of the places where Christians as citizens take their civic bearings.

Lurking in the interstices is a major fissure, even schism, in contemporary church life, namely, the gap between the pulpit and the pew. I think of this often when I hear a pastor or minister intone matter-of-factly against capital punishment, against the use of force even in a just case (presumably there is always an effective alternative), for the current administration's "universal health care," and the like. But Christians disagree on these matters. One knows there is by no means unanimity in these issues in the pews. But the pew-folks have no way to articulate their differences with the pulpit. So there is murmuring and grumbling, but little chance to explore why and how Christians might disagree.

The Christian Difference

Our houses of worship should be places where a "Christian difference" is named because Christians are claimed by hope. This surely includes the cultural critics among us, although one would scarcely know that, given the remarkable absence of charity in much cultural criticism issuing forth from many Christian commentators over the past decade or so. Let me offer up three points for our consideration. I trust you will see their direct connection to any project of cultural criticism with a "Christian difference." One must be prepared to offer a reasoned defense of one's position and to engage interlocutors from a stance of openness tethered to an insistence that there is some truth to be found. Now more than ever, Christians as citizens must be defenders of human reason, insistent that epistemological questions cannot be severed from ontological concerns if the complexity of truth is to be approached.

A second difference those who call themselves Christians can and should make is to roll back the curtain of modern meaninglessness. That means to display what incarnational being-in-the-world is all about. We are called to cultivate citizens who make visible before the world the fullness, dignity, and wonder of creation—and horror, then, at its wanton destruction. For modern deadness is all around us—the conviction that the world is so much matter to manipulate; that abstract signs and symbols entirely of our own creation that can be sent whirring around the globe in milliseconds are the reality that counts.

Christianity, by contrast, is a remarkably enfleshed way of being. If one takes embodiment seriously, the dignity of the ensouled body, there are implications for many of our so-called rights, the "right to die," the right to abortion on demand, and so on. The Christian will likely put himself at odds with the cultural mainstream, but better this than capitulating entirely to the Zeitgeist.

A third charge that Christians who live in hope must assure is that their churches play a critical role as interpreters of the culture to the culture. This is a critical civic task. There are few such sites available. One imagines a "Jesus Goes to the Oscar" night where what is discussed is the state of contemporary cinema. There could be discussions of economic issues, social issues, how Christians can and should handle deep differences in their own ranks, and so on. The social ministries are vital. But these civic-critical efforts should also be mounted.

We also need to teach, to model, and to practice solitude, a rich alone-ness, where one is never truly alone. It was at Ettal Monastery, some may recall, that Dietrich Bonhoeffer found the necessary solitude to complete major portions of what remained his unfinished ethics. It is too bad, really, that Protestants gave up on monastic and conventual life of the sort that lifts up solitude with and among others, sociality with silence, prayer and group reflection, the sharing of rituals.

In Robert Bolt's *A Man for All Seasons,* Thomas More, speaking to his beloved daughter, Meg, proclaims that God created human beings to serve Him wittily in the tangle of their minds.[7] I submit that we are not doing an awfully good job of serving in this way. We need to quicken and enliven our minds; to nurture the reflective possibilities that the wider culture seems systematically hell-bent on destroying or squeezing out of human life. I know it is always a temptation of critics to make things worse than they are in order to highlight their own heroic efforts to make things right. One must avoid this self-heroization by remembering that the connected critic is not a hero but a citizen among citizens, a fellow laborer in the vineyard. And that is as it should be.

Notes

1. H. Richard Niebuhr, *Christ and Culture* (New York: Harper and Row, 1951).

2. See Jean Bethke Elshtain, "With or Against Culture?" *Christianity Today International,* October 12, 2006.

3. Martin Luther King's speech "I've Been to the Mountaintop," April 3, 1968.

4. Michael Walzer, *The Company Critics: Social Criticism and Political Commitment in the 20th Century* (New York: Basic Books, 2002).

5. Frederick Douglass, "The Slave Holders' Rebellion," Rochester, NY, July 4, 1862.

6. Benedict Carey, "Use of Antipsychotics by the Young Rose Fivefold," *New York Times,* June 6, 2006.

7. Robert Bolt, *A Man for All Seasons* (New York: Random House, 1962).

PART 3

THE POSSIBILITIES OF CULTURAL CHANGE

TWO CITIES, HOW MANY CULTURES?

Ken Myers

In 1939, just before England entered World War II, T.S. Eliot gave three lectures at Cambridge that were later assembled in an essay entitled "The Idea of a Christian Society." There are numerous brilliant observations in that essay, but I would like to begin my essay by focusing on one sentence: "The fact that a problem will certainly take a long time to solve, and that it will demand the attention of many minds for several generations, is no justification for postponing the study."[1]

I offer that as a starting point because I believe the problems present in American culture are not problems that can be fixed easily or quickly. They will demand the attention of many minds—and many hearts and bodies—for several generations. The cultural challenges we face are a function of—among other things—a long legacy of thinking about how the sacred and the secular interact in American culture, thinking that in turn has shaped the formation of the dominant institutions of our culture. The future of American culture can be fruitfully addressed only in light of certain aspects of its past and its present, aspects that I believe offer a particular challenge to Christian citizens in America. The argument I'll make is both theological and sociological, an argument primarily about the nature and calling of the church in the world and secondarily about how cultures are shaped and how they shape their members. Reducing my argument to a single sentence, I want to suggest that American Christians can best serve the health of American culture by striving to be deliberate about and faithful to a way of life that Robert Wilken has called the culture of the city of God.[2]

THE CHURCH VERSUS THE CULTURE

Not long ago I interviewed a poet who—during a rambling conversation about art and the church and creativity and language—ended up musing about the life of the early church, specifically about how Christians in the first few centuries of the church's life regarded the culture around them. He suggested that he just couldn't imagine early church leaders sitting around trying to come up with clever ideas about how they might influence Roman culture. Church historian Robert Wilken made a very similar comment in an interview given in 1998 in which he reflected on the early church's posture toward its cultural surroundings. Wilken pointed out that the principal way the early church leaders sustained cultural influence was by discipling church members, by conveying to them that the call of the Gospel was a call to embrace a new way of life. The church was less interested in transforming the disorders of the Roman Empire than in building "its own sense of community, and it let these communities be the leaven that would gradually transform culture." The church was not a body that "spoke to its culture; it was itself a culture and created a new Christian culture."[3]

That same point was made in a conversation I had several years ago with D.H. Williams, now a professor at Baylor University who teaches the works of the early church fathers. We talked about how seriously the early church's supervision of new converts took this process of enculturating its members.

> In the process of teaching, or catechizing new Christians [Williams said to me], it was taken with great seriousness that the commitment that they were making was a corporate one, and an exclusive one. And that it entailed a body of meaning that in many ways was inviting them to become members of a counterculture, from the one in which they had converted from. And even the catechetical process itself begins to raise important questions about the church as culture. That you are de facto encouraging the new Christian to learn a new vocabulary, a new sense of what is the highest, the good, and the beautiful; that there really are true things

and false things; that there really are certain moral lines to be drawn in the sand, and that you may struggle with these, and part of the struggle is very good.[4]

To speak of the church as a culture is to use the word *culture* in a thicker way than it is often used today. When Robert Wilken writes of a Christian culture, he means the "pattern of inherited meanings and sensibilities encoded in rituals, law, language, practices, and stories that can order, inspire, and guide the behavior, thoughts, and affections of a Christian people."[5] By referring to "a Christian people," Wilken is reminding individualistic Americans that the Gospel is about the calling of *a people,* not the making of discrete and separate converts. This view permeates the New Testament; using language that echoes texts in the Torah, Saint Peter addresses Christian exiles in Asia Minor (and future generations of Christian believers) this way: "You are a chosen race, a royal priesthood, a holy nation, a people for his own possession, that you may proclaim the excellencies of him who called you out of darkness into his marvelous light. Once you were not a people, but now you are God's people; once you had not received mercy, but now you have received mercy."[6]

Theologian Peter Leithart has picked up on this theme in arguing, "In the New Testament, we do not find an essentially private gospel being applied to the public sphere, as if the public implications of the gospel were a second story built on the private ground floor. The gospel is the announcement of the Father's formation, through His Son and the Spirit, of a new city—the city of God."[7]

If this is the case, Leithart argues, then "the Church is not a club for religious people. The Church is a way of living together before God, a new way of being human together." This was surely the perspective of the early church, but one wonders how common it is today. The assemblies of believers in the first century and long after were not perceived to be resource centers for the promotion of merely private spirituality; they were not religious branches of the larger Greco-Roman project. Rather, the early church lived with the formative conviction "that God has established the eschatological order of human life in the midst of history, not perfectly but truly." Therefore, the church's life—the shared relationships and practices

of the redeemed community—was truly a matter with public consequences. Leithart argues that these public consequences reflect the
eschatological character of the church. "The Church anticipates the
form of the human race as it will be when it comes to maturity; she is
the 'already' of the new humanity that will be perfected in the 'not yet'
of the last day." So conversion necessarily led to discipleship that had
extensive consequences. "Conversion thus means turning from one
way of life, one culture, to another. Conversion is the beginning of a
'resocialization,' . . . and 'inculturation' into the way of life practiced
by the eschatological community."[8]

A Lost Vision

Modern Christianity has largely lost sight of this vision. We assume
that our way of life will be substantially shaped not by the Gospel, but
by the convictions and practices dictated by government, the market, science, technology, and popular entertainment. Our churches
are quite likely to be low-commitment clubs for religious people
rather than definitive communities of disciples striving to live all of
life under God's kingship. For many modern Christians, churches are
dispensers of eternal security and uplift—fire insurance and mood
brighteners—not nurturers of a whole way of life, not the source of
the best ways to act and think in all spheres of experience. The message of the Gospel is commonly assumed to be personal and private,
not communal and public. So many well-meaning Christians believe
that the best way for the church to influence American culture is by
imitating as much as possible whatever way of life happens to be fash-
ionable and popular, in the hopes that people will like us and listen to
us. What we have for America is a message about an ethereal eternal
life and about coping with frustrations here and now, and so we just
need to communicate a message about a short list of values capable of
being perceived as relevant to conventional lifestyles.

The assumption that we can compartmentalize abstract values
from a concrete way of life—embodied in practices and institutions—is part of our problem. It ignores the essential links between
what we believe, what we love, and how we live in the world as embodied creatures. Our deepest convictions (which often involve in-

tertwined beliefs and moral commitments) are both cause and effect of the way we live. Love for neighbors, for example, leads to a way of life in which the interests of neighbors are honored. Such a way of life faithfully passed on from generation to generation will build into our children the proper dispositions and beliefs. Ideas have consequences, and they also have antecedents in specific practices. It is a mistake to believe that traditional values can be sustained without traditions. Our heads often follow our hearts; we believe what we love believing. And our hearts are often shaped by how we live as embodied creatures. A culture cultivates its most fundamental convictions by sustaining practices that shape our loves and so guide our thinking.

Richard Weaver, in the first chapter of *Ideas Have Consequences* makes a similar (and very Augustinian) observation: "When we affirm that philosophy begins with wonder, we are affirming in effect that sentiment is anterior to reason. We do not undertake to reason about anything until we have been drawn to it by an affective interest." I have heard that Weaver did not like the title *Ideas Have Consequences* for his book; perhaps *Ideas Have Antecedents* would have been a better title. The very first paragraph in chapter 1 makes it clear that Weaver wasn't just interested in the *effects* ideas have, but in the convictions, the dispositions that *sustain* ideas. "Every man participating in a culture has three levels of conscious reflection: his specific ideas about things, his general beliefs or convictions, and his metaphysical dream of the world." By "metaphysical dream" he means the intuitive sense we have of the way the world is, not a set of theoretical constructions, but a deep, precognitive world-picture. Later, he writes, "Culture is originally a matter of yea-saying" and "Culture is sentiment refined and measured by intellect."[9]

Weaver's observation that our explicit ideas rest on what he calls a metaphysical dream echoes nicely with Philip Rieff's description of how cultures shape consciousness and conscience, described in *The Triumph of the Therapeutic*. "A culture survives principally, I think, by the power of its institutions to bind and loose men in the conduct of their affairs with reasons which sink so deep into the self that they become commonly and implicitly understood—with that understanding of which explicit belief and precise knowledge of externals would show outwardly like the tip of an iceberg."[10]

In *To Change the World,* sociologist James Davison Hunter similarly points out that a culture is a system of truth claims and moral obligations embedded within narratives, within myths, within practices that shape the moral imagination. A culture is a worldview, but in a much deeper sense than that word is usually used. "This 'worldview' is so deeply embedded in our consciousness, in the habits of our lives, and in our social practices that to question one's worldview is to question reality itself."[11]

When one has the sense that one belongs to a moral community, moral conformity is not simply a bare duty, the taking of a heroic and isolated stand. Rather, uprightness is expected and rewarded by a rich network of social relationships. In a true community, a person is and feels like a member of something, and that membership carries with it certain comforts and certain expectations.

Fear of ostracism isn't the only factor at work. A moral code that is shared by one's fellows gains in its plausibility. A belief in sexual chastity, if shared in a matter-of-fact way by a body of people who have the sense of *being* a "people," has the intuitive sense of being *the way things are*—not just the rule of "our sort of folks" but the very texture of creation itself. The deep plausibility of values communally sustained forms and deepens a conscientious sense of doing the right thing, which (in tandem with external pressures) serves as a powerful restraint on licentious behavior. In such a setting, an affection for good behavior is possible as people are not only afraid to do what is wrong but ashamed of it as well.

So far, I've offered a theological claim and a sociological/anthropological observation. First, the church is best understood as a community sustaining a way of life informed by truth claims rather than an agency committed to transmitting truth claims that don't require any particular way of life. That picture of the church is a claim that the Gospel is not a message about *escaping* human existence but about the *redemption* of human life and a call to live out that life now and into eternity in concrete, public ways. Second (and related to the view of the church as a community) is the sociological claim that moral life is necessarily rooted in and sustained by community. What we believe, what we claim as knowledge, is guided by an antecedent orientation of the heart or of the soul, and the role of cultural institutions in our lives is to orient our affections—to shape our pretheoretical convictions about what kinds of beings we are, what kind of world we live in, and what way of life would be adequate to suit the nature of things. Such convictions are sustained not principally by argument (as Enlightenment thinkers would prefer), but by participation in a community, by being members of a body.

THE CHURCH AND CULTURAL DISORDER

If these claims are true, then the best way American Christians can serve their neighbors is to be willing to commit to a richly different way of life than is currently conventional. This requires recognizing cultural disorder that isn't obviously moral. A good example of this kind of disorder is the rise in the mid-twentieth century of what we call "youth culture," with its assumption that intergenerational discontinuity is the norm. Given that culture rightly understood is an intergenerational system of communicating moral convictions, the very term *youth culture* should be seen as a contradiction in terms.

Marketers have successfully entrenched the notion of youth culture by creating product lines that are intended to define adolescent identity as a deliberate rejection of parental expectations. Not only does this age segregation weaken the family's ability to pursue the cultural task of moral transmission; it also weakens the understanding of the family itself. A proper understanding of the meaning of family is intergenerational *in all directions*. In considering the role of the family in shaping culture, T.S. Eliot was careful to point out that he thought even the nuclear family was much too limited a scope: "When I speak of the family, I have in mind a bond which embraces a longer period of time than this [that is, the living members of a nuclear family]: a piety toward the dead, however obscure, and a solicitude for the unborn, however remote. Unless this reverence for past and future is cultivated in the home, it can never be more than a verbal convention in the community."[12] The dynamics of youth culture segregate generations and extol the experience of the present at the expense of honoring the past and preparing for the future. Youth culture isn't good for culture. It is a form of disorder. And yet it is a form that American churches were quick to embrace, apparently because they believed that adapting to the form of youth culture was an effective way to communicate a message of salvation. The questions of whether or not it offered a good way to live life, of whether or not it was culturally healthy and sustaining, don't seem to have been of great concern to many church and parachurch leaders for the past sixty years or so.

This blithe indifference to cultural forms and their consequences is encouraged by the assumption in modern American Christianity—an assumption that is rooted in the Enlightenment more than in scripture or in the church's premodern history—that the Gospel is an essentially private and personal message, with minimal cultural consequences. The assumption of Enlightenment thinkers was that public life—including government, commerce, science, artistic pursuits, and much of education—could be organized according to the discoveries of allegedly unaided reason *without* reference to revelation or tradition. Religion was private and subjective. Over time, this viewpoint has become the dominant view in the West.

It is odd that most Christians behave as if this Enlightenment view of religion were valid. As a result, many devout American Christians for a long time believed that being too interested in cultural matters, paying very much attention to the shape of cultural institutions, was a distraction from the real focus of Christian life. So beginning in the nineteenth century, many American Christians were culturally indifferent and culturally inert. In education, for example, for decades, a secularizing view of education was taking hold of American public schools, and Christians rarely noticed. Ideas about the nature of knowledge and the nature of learning that were quite a departure from historic Christian thinking were influencing the way teaching was conducted in this country, and Christians (at least, Protestants, both mainline and evangelical) just kept sending their kids to public schools. Only in the 1960s, when school prayer was declared unconstitutional, did Christians suddenly care about public education. That is, only when an explicitly religious issue became obvious did Christians get upset.

The same is true in other areas of cultural life. For centuries, the ideas that science has promoted about the nature of knowledge, the nature of nature, and the nature of human nature have been moving farther and farther away from a recognizably Christian understanding of such matters. For example, science promoted a mechanical model of nature and of human nature that had significantly dehumanizing consequences. But Christians generally ignored what science was doing *until* evolution became a big issue in schools, evolution being perceived as posing problems about the authority of the Bible.

In the arts, Christians generally ignored trends for the past two hundred years; they only got upset when André Serrano put a crucifix in a vat of urine with National Endowment for the Arts funding or when Robert Mapplethorpe's homoerotic photographs (also NEA-supported) were celebrated. Only when the arts transgress a line toward the explicitly religious or obviously moral have Christians taken much notice.

In literature, Christians today generally ignore the substance and form of contemporary fiction in both popular and more literary work. But when books like *The Da Vinci Code* or the Harry Potter novels come along—books that make explicitly religious claims—Christians take notice. Never mind that other very popular books might advance all sorts of bad ideas about all sorts of matters, such as the nature of work or of history or of language or of personal identity, matters concerning which Christians should have an interest.

In business, we have seen in the past century the rise of several influential theories about the nature of work and of management. Some of these have been, from the standpoint of a Christian worldview, very troubling. We have also seen a number of changes in the shape of capitalism that would have bothered Augustine, or Aquinas, or Calvin, or Wesley. But for the most part, as long as Christian businessmen have the freedom to have Bible studies and witness to their colleagues, it's business as usual.

In the world of sports, many thoughtful secular critics over the past few decades have lamented the loss of play and of sportsmanship as professional sports have become more commercialized, more commodified, more driven by the demands of television. There have been a few thoughtful Christian academic works on these matters, but the only critical response I've noticed from Christians at a popular level toward changes in the world of sports was the outcry a few years back, when the NFL said it was going to prohibit churches from having SuperBowl parties.

THE CHURCH AND TIME

Moving beyond disorders within specific cultural spheres to more general tendencies that are evident in many cultural settings, consider conventional attitudes and practices regarding our understanding of time. How people perceive time—and how cultural forms order the experience of time—is a central feature of human cultures, one that can orient perceptions of larger realities. Cultures that affirm the reality of a Creator who has ordered time in some way will enact that affirmation in their temporal practices. Cultures that are based on the assumption that nature is a random and meaningless assemblage of inherently insignificant stuff will treat time more pragmatically or mechanistically. Until the modern period, Christians were quite conscious of how they measured, marked, and ritualized time. After all, the scriptures present us with a divinely shaped cosmos in which human beings are meant to enjoy the rhythms of creation. Long before giving the command to keep the Sabbath, God established an anthropocentric rhythm in the solar system, creating the sun and the moon and the stars "for signs and for seasons, and for days and years" (Gen. 1:14, ESV). The sun and the moon are identified as rulers, assigned a specific dominion, long before man is given viceregency.

The observance of the Sabbath (and subsequently of what came to be known as the "Christian Sabbath") is a singular instance of a general pattern of acknowledging that time has meaning, a pattern observed by all human cultures before the advent of modernity. The post-Christian character of modern culture is evidenced in the denial—in theory and in practice—that the cosmos has any inherent patterns that societies would do well to observe. Our lives are now lived 24/7; the pursuit of convenience and efficiency is more valued by our culture (and by us) than the recognition and symbolic honoring of any cosmic order. And as our arbitrary and egocentric ordering of time becomes more vital to us than God's structuring of it, the church itself comes to be guided by efficiency instead of divine order.

Time has been ordered by God. This is one of the church's fundamental claims. Do our lives reflect that created reality? I think American Christians are much more willing to fight about the *fact* of Creation (against Darwinism) or fight with one another about how many hours Creation took than they are to order their lives around the structure that God has placed *in* creation. Contemporary American Christians want to insist on the fact of Creation even as they consistently ignore the meaning and significance of the order of Creation.

DANGERS OF DUALISM

There is a bigger dualistic pattern evident here. Many modern Christians commonly assume that there is a compartment of life called "religion"—principally concerned with personal and family matters—and that Jesus is Lord over that realm of experience. The other spheres of life—the world of culture, including economics, science, education, politics, technology, art: human life in space and time beyond the narrow slice of internal experience we call religion—is not something Jesus really cares much about, as long as general principles of morality are observed.

The Lord of Heaven and Earth has been reduced to the Lord of private life. It is popularly assumed by many devout Christians that Jesus cares about our souls but not about all of the settings within which our minds and bodies are actively engaged.

By accepting this dualistic marginalization of religion—by reading the New Testament as a guide to a merely private faith—American Christians have left a vacuum now filled by other (post-Christian) institutional forces. Modern cultures make a bargain with Christians: we'll give you religious freedom as long as you don't use that freedom to influence cultural institutions in any way that contradicts the assumptions of modernity. Surely, it is a good thing to be allowed to worship and preach without interference. Indeed, modern ideas of religious freedom are the product of (among other things) a Christian understanding of human dignity. But the logic of the modern bargain has resulted in a faith that is not only culturally inert but culturally captive. When Christians lose sight of the fact that the Gospel calls them to a way of life—whether or not their neighbors like it—they very easily fall captive to the conventional way of life of the surrounding society. This is not, of course, a new problem: it is a story repeated throughout the Bible.

THE CHURCH AND MORAL AUTHORITY

Modern culture in general—and modern American culture in particular—has unfolded since at least the Enlightenment guided by a small set of assumptions about reality. Sociologist Daniel Bell has summarized the modern mentality as one dedicated to "the proposition that there are no ends or purposes given in nature; that the individual, and his or her self-realization, is the new standard of judgement." There is, Bell goes on to argue, a single theme that focuses all of the distinctively modern movements in culture: "the rejection of a revealed order or natural order, and the substitution of the individual—the ego, the self—as the lodestar of consciousness. . . . There are no doubts about the moral authority of the self; that is simply taken as a given. The only question is what constitutes fulfillment of the self."[13]

Most American Christians would probably object to these modern axioms. But I don't believe the cultural lives of Christians—and the increasingly consumer-oriented pattern of the programs of modern churches—are effectively bearing witness to our moral imaginations that there are, in fact, purposes embedded in the very shape of creation. When churches order their cultural life to mimic the patterns of a society composed of sovereign selves, there is less and less opportunity for our neighbors to imagine that this modern view of the cosmos might be false. We thus fail our Lord and our neighbors.

Let me cite as evidence of this failure some of the findings in a recent book by Notre Dame sociologist Christian Smith: *Souls in Transition: The Religious and Spiritual Lives of Emerging Adults.* The term *emerging adults* was a new one to me. It is apparently now a fixture among social scientists. Long ago, societies were composed of children and adults. In the twentieth century, life was segmented into three periods: childhood, adolescence, and adulthood. Now—thanks to a combination of social and cultural factors, including the effects of a globalized economy, the deterioration of cultural conventions defining adulthood, and the remarkable popularity of online role-playing games—we now have a fourth phase in the life cycle: emerging adulthood, a long, uncertain period that may last from late teens to late twenties.

Christian Smith's book is a sequel to an earlier study he wrote on the spiritual and religious lives of American teenagers. Many of the emerging adults he and his colleagues interviewed for this new book have been under gentle surveillance for some years now, and the lessons learned from this study are a bit frightening. Let me cite some conclusions from a chapter called "The Cultural Worlds of Emerging Adults."

> The majority of emerging adults . . . have great difficulty grasping the idea that a reality that is objective to their own awareness or construction of it may exist that could have a significant bearing on their lives. In philosophical terms, most emerging adults functionally (meaning how they actually think and act, regardless of the theories they hold) are soft ontological antirealists and epistemological skeptics and perspectivalists—although few have any conscious idea what those terms mean. They seem to presuppose that they are simply imprisoned in their own subjective selves, limited to their biased interpretations of their own sense perceptions, unable to know the real truth of anything beyond themselves. They are de facto doubtful that an identifiable, objective, shared reality might exist across and around people that can serve as a reliable reference point for rational deliberation and argument. So, for example, when we interviewers tried to get respondents to talk about whether what they take to be substantive moral beliefs reflect some objective or universal quality or standard [or] are simply relative human inventions, many—if not most—could not understand what we interviewers were trying to get at. They had difficulty seeing the possible distinction between, in this case, objective moral truth and relative human invention. This is not because they are dumb. It seems to be because they cannot, for whatever reason, believe in—or sometimes even conceive of—a given, objective truth, fact, reality, or nature of the world that is independent of their subjective self-experience and that in relation to which they and others might learn or be persuaded to change. Although none would put it in exactly this way, what emerging adults take to be reality ultimately seems to consist

of a multitude of subjective but ultimately autonomous experiences. People are thus trying to communicate with each other in order to simply be able to get along and enjoy life as they see fit. Beyond that, anything truly objectively shared or common or real seems impossible to access.[14]

Those of us who are eager to make public arguments about moral issues by appealing to the idea of natural law need to acknowledge that natural law is an increasingly implausible—indeed, nonsensical—concept. I believe it to be a valid concept, but there is almost nothing in public life—including in the observable life of many churches—that would inform the moral imaginations of twentysomethings (and younger) of what could be meant by "natural law."

If natural law is nonsense and the sovereign self is the lodestar of all moral life, it would not be surprising to learn that most emerging adults believe that moral decision making is remarkably simple. This is exactly what Christian Smith reports, under the heading "Right and Wrong Are Easy": "The majority of emerging adults interviewed had difficulty thinking of even one example of a situation recently when they had some trouble deciding what was the morally right or wrong thing to do. Most of those who finally did come up with an example pointed to the moral and emotional difficulty they had in deciding whether or not to break up with a boyfriend or girlfriend. In short, thinking and living morally is quite effortless—you merely pay attention to your inner self, and it all comes fairly naturally."[15]

If right and wrong are assumed to be easy, we should not be surprised when we encounter impatience with extended moral reasoning. One could hope that at least our churches could still be places where one could hear sermons that actually make somewhat developed moral arguments. But that will require sustaining within the church a culture of reason that would appear to be remarkably unfashionable and irrelevant.

Under the heading "Everybody's Different," Smith notes that most emerging adults believe that

humans share very little in common with each other, that you don't count on any common features or interests across people that bind them together or give them a basis on which to work on disagreements. And the differences emphasized are not merely cross-cultural dissimilarities between, say, American and Chinese. As in well-known postmodern-ist theory, the differences actually drive down to individual personalities. Any given person has his or her own unique beliefs, tastes, feelings, thoughts, desires, and expectations. Nobody can presume to impose on or perhaps even fully understand those of another. Literally every individual is different. . . . And so interviewers heard them saying things like "I think the last few years have made me more aware of [how] what's right for me may be wrong for someone else or what's wrong for me may be okay for somebody else. I think it's made me more aware of other people's feelings about things." Concerning religious faith, one said, "You know, the Muslim religion is not right for me, but it doesn't make it wrong for them. I just think it's subjective to each person. I really do think that everything is pretty subjective."[16]

The assumption that morality is entirely idiosyncratic will make it increasingly difficult to make public appeals to any notion of the common good. Again, churches have a great opportunity to be living witnesses that communities dedicated to sustaining a common no-tion of the good are not thereby tyrannical and ugly.

The next section of Smith's summary is called "It's Up to the Individual."

It is hardly surprising, in light of much of the foregoing, that according to emerging adults, the absolute authority for ev-ery person's beliefs or actions is his or her own sovereign self. Anybody can literally think or do whatever he or she wants. Of course, what a person chooses to think or do may have bad consequences for that person. But everything is ulti-mately up to each individual to decide for himself or herself. The most one should ever do toward influencing another person is to ask him or her to consider what one thinks. No-body is bound to any course of action by virtue of belonging to a group or because of a common good. Individuals are autonomous agents who have to deal with each other, yes, but do so entirely as self-directing choosers. The words duty, responsibility, and obligation feel somehow vaguely coercive or puritanical.[17]

Now, one might hear these summaries and conclude that these widespread assumptions are the effect of postmodern relativists let loose in our schools. And that is partly true. But I would argue that most of these young people—long before they heard lectures on respecting diversity—had already been oriented toward this sort of subjectivism by the absorption of a kind of cultural style that Mark Edmundson calls the "cool consumer worldview."

> I think that many of [my students] have imbibed their sense of self from consumer culture in general and from the tube in particular. They're the progeny of 100 cable channels and omnipresent Blockbuster outlets. TV, Marshall McLuhan famously said, is a cool medium. Those who play best on it are low-key and nonassertive; they blend in. Enthusiasm . . . quickly looks absurd. The form of character that's most appealing on TV is calmly self-interested though never greedy, attuned to the conventions, and ironic. Judicious timing is preferred to sudden self-assertion. The TV medium is inhospitable to inspiration, improvisation, failures, slipups. All must run perfectly.[18]

THE NEED: A COUNTERCULTURAL CHURCH

A cultural style that lacks the possibility of earnestness—that suggests there's nothing really worth being earnest about—has become increasingly common, especially in the past twenty or thirty years. When church leaders in America mimic cool cultural styles—both in personal demeanor and in the forms of public gatherings—in the interest of making their message about salvation and eternal life more attractive, they fail to see that the medium is often the dominating message. When churches are encouraged to think of themselves as marketers of a product and to act accordingly, they cast those they serve into the role of consumers—*sovereign* customers rather than humble disciples. And that in turn establishes an orientation of the heart that is very hard to redirect. Many clergy and parachurch leaders don't even try to challenge this cool posture for fear of losing market share.

I have been suggesting that the best service churches can offer American culture is to be properly countercultural. Presbyterian pastor and teacher Eugene Peterson has argued, "It is the task of the Christian community to give witness and guidance in the living of life in a culture that is relentless in reducing, constricting, and enervating life."[19] Similarly, Robert Wilken has suggested, "At this moment in the Church's history in this country (and in the West more generally) it is less urgent to convince the alternative culture in which we live of the truth of Christ than it is for the Church to tell itself its own story and to nurture its own life, the culture of the city of God."[20]

In a 1995 interview, Joseph Cardinal Ratzinger put forth the following hypothesis:

> Perhaps the time has come to say farewell to the idea of traditionally Catholic cultures. Maybe we are facing a new and different kind of epoch in the Church's history, where Christianity will again be characterized more by the mustard seed, where it will exist in small seemingly insignificant groups that nonetheless live an intensive struggle against evil and bring the good into the world—that let God in. . . . If society in its totality is no longer a Christian environment, just as it was not in the first four or five centuries, the Church herself must form cells in which mutual support and a common journey, and thus the great vital milieu of the church in miniature, can be experienced and put into practice. . . . The Church of tomorrow . . . will be a Church of minority.[21]

This is not a matter of abandoning the world or our neighbors; it is to recognize the very biblical theme that we are called to be *against* the world *for* the world. In using that phrase, I am honoring the work of a group of eighteen scholars and clerics who, in 1975, gathered in

Hartford, Connecticut, to discuss various ways in which American Christianity had become captive to the spirit of the age. They presented a series of papers later published in a book entitled *Against the World For the World* and a manifesto called the Hartford Appeal. In the words of the Appeal, "The renewal of Christian witness and mission requires constant examination of the assumptions shaping the Church's life. Today an apparent loss of a sense of the transcendent is undermining the Church's ability to address with clarity and courage the urgent tasks to which God calls it in the world. This loss is manifest in a number of pervasive themes. Many are superficially attractive, but upon closer examination we find these themes false and debilitating to the Church's life and work."[22]

One of the signers of the Hartford Appeal was theologian Stanley Hauerwas, then teaching at Notre Dame and now teaching at Duke. In 1995 Hauerwas wrote an article very much in the spirit of the Hartford Appeal, called "Preaching as Though We Had Enemies." He said, "One hopes that God is using this time to remind the Church that Christianity is unintelligible without enemies. Indeed the whole point of Christianity is to produce the right kind of enemies."[23]

If modern Christians hope to have a positive influence in American culture, they need to think long and hard about how to make the right sort of enemies (making enemies as such is not hard, but it's not always easy to have the right enemies). Of course, some Christians are reluctant to admit that they *should* have enemies. After all, since we must *love* our enemies, actually *having* enemies would require loving someone who might be really nasty to us. It's a lot easier to behave in a way that avoids making enemies, no matter what compromises we need to make, just so long as we don't actually have to love someone who is out to do us in. We would all rather *be* loved than have to *love* an enemy. But Jesus calls us to love God more than to love being loved. And loving God will, in a twisted world, produce enemies. Loving justice more than profit may produce enemies. Loving truth more than power may produce enemies. Loving the law of love itself more than loving the principle of self-indulgence may produce enemies. But only as the church imitates Christ this way can we hope to be the witness and example that American culture so desperately needs.

NOTES

1. T.S. Eliot, "The Idea of a Christian Society," in *Christianity and Culture* (New York: Harcourt Brace Jovanovich, 1968), 5.

2. Robert Louis Wilken, "The Church as Culture," *First Things,* April 2004, www.firstthings.com/article/2008/02/the-church-as-culture-12.

3. Robert Louis Wilken, "Evangelism in the Early Church: Christian History Interview—Roman Redux," *Christian History,* issue 57 (1998), www.christianitytoday.com/ch/1998/issue57/57h042.html?

4. *Mars Hill Audio Journal,* vol. 76 (2005), available from http://marshillaudio.org.

5. Wilken, "Church as Culture."

6. 1 Peter 2:9–10, ESV.

7. Peter J. Leithart, *Against Christianity* (Moscow, ID: Canon Press, 2003), 16.

8. Ibid.

9. Richard M. Weaver, *Ideas Have Consequences* (Chicago: Univ. of Chicago Press, 1948), 19, 18, 19, 23.

10. Philip Rieff, *The Triumph of the Therapeutic: Uses of Faith after Freud* (Chicago: Univ. of Chicago Press, 1966), 2–3.

11. James Davison Hunter, *To Change the World: The Irony, Tragedy, and Possibility of Christianity in the Late Modern World* (New York: Oxford Univ. Press, 2010), 33.

12. Eliot, "The Idea of a Christian Society," 116.

13. Daniel Bell, "Resolving the Contradictions of Modernity and Modernism," *Society* 27, no. 3 (March–April 1990): 43, 45–46.

14. Christian Smith with Patricia Snell, *Souls in Transition: The Religious and Spiritual Lives of Emerging Adults* (New York: Oxford Univ. Press, 2009), 45–46.

15. Ibid., 46.

16. Ibid., 48–49.

17. Ibid., 49.

18. Mark Edmundson, "On the Uses of a Liberal Education," *Harper's,* September 1997, 41.

19. Eugene Peterson, *Christ Plays in Ten Thousand Places: A Conversation in Spiritual Theology* (Grand Rapids: Eerdmans, 2005), 3.

20. Wilken, "Church as Culture."

21. Joseph Cardinal Ratzinger, *Salt of the Earth: The Church at the End of the Millennium—an Interview with Peter Seewal* (San Francisco: Ignatius Press, 1998), 16, 265.

22. Peter L. Berger, ed., *Against the World For the World: The Hartford Appeal and the Future of American Religion* (New York: Seabury Press, 1976), 1.

23. Stanley Hauerwas, "Preaching as Though We Had Enemies," *First Things,* May 1995, 47.

SOURCES OF RENEWAL IN TWENTY-FIRST-CENTURY AMERICA

Wilfred M. McClay

These past few years have been a rough and discouraging stretch for Americans in general, and perhaps especially for American conservatives. Yet in such times all of us should recall the counsel of Shakespeare, expressed by the exiled and deposed Duke Senior in *As You Like It*:

> Sweet are the uses of adversity,
> Which, like the toad, ugly and venomous,
> Wears yet a precious jewel in his head. (act 2, scene 1, lines 12–14)

There is, in other words, something to be said for the sheer gravity of the challenges we now face as a nation, challenges that we can no longer evade or postpone. Their weightiness may even turn out to be a providential gift, albeit one shrouded in deep and unattractive disguise.

Arnold Toynbee saw the dynamic of challenge-and-response as the chief source of a civilization's greatness. Far from being the fruit of a steady inner-directed maturation, a civilization's higher development arose out of its skill and stamina in overcoming a succession of ordeals. "Creation," he asserted, "is the outcome of an encounter," and "genesis is a product of interaction."[1] Great civilizations die from suicide rather than murder, which is to say that they die when they no longer possess the will to respond confidently and creatively to the very challenges that would otherwise make them stronger and better.

He was right. Challenge and response is the way of life—and the way of national renewal. The challenges facing us are so great now, as we look at our massive and unsustainable deficits, our faltering economy, our fragile families and fraying moral fabric, and our diminishing place in the world, that we have no choice but to respond to them. The gravity of the situation forces us to think our way back to our first principles. This is not quite what President Obama's chief of staff Rahm Emanuel had in mind when he spoke his now-famous words—probably the chief ones for which history will remember him—"You never want a serious crisis to go to waste." But we would be doing just that, wasting the crisis by failing to learn from it, were we to respond with acts of mere band-aid pragmatism and temporizing.

OBAMA AND CULTURAL CHANGE

Some think the way to respond is to ramp up the comprehensive supervisory power of our cultural elites, and of the political class that embodies and serves them, over our society and economy. This is the view of the Obama administration, with its centralized and technocratic vision of social reform and its stress on the uses of expert knowledge in the proper governance of human affairs—ideas that are far from new but rather are throwbacks to the central contention of the Progressive movement of a hundred years ago and a clear gesture in the direction of the vast, all-embracing, and severely strained welfare states of northwestern Europe. It is also the view of figures like *New York Times* columnist David Brooks, who has warmly embraced the Obama administration, praised its "pragmatism" and reliance upon "professional expertise," and admonished conservatives for choosing to "stick with Reagan" in perpetuating an "insane" antagonism to a large and powerful national government.[2]

What we are seeing is the latest installment in a long-running theme of modern American history: the dream of *technocracy,* meaning the rule of society by accredited and academically certified experts, disinterested authorities who in turn direct an enveloping web of bureaucrats, engineers, civil servants, and other professionals and technicians employed by a vastly enlarged and all-embracing state apparatus. This was the lofty dream of philosophes and utopians such as Marquis de Condorcet and Auguste Comte and Lester Frank Ward, who believed that, given the intelligibility of the world and the limitless capacity of human reason, the methods of science should be extended to embrace all aspects of life, including the ordering and administration of social and political affairs.

The idea, in full or partial form, has had many exponents over the years, even in democratic America. It informed the shape and direction taken by the professions—medical, legal, scientific, scholarly—that established themselves as bastions of expertise in the last decades of the nineteenth century. It has held a particular attraction for those who dislike or distrust the activity of democratic politics, with its rough and tumble clash of competing interests, ideologies, and passions and its susceptibility to corruption and dishonesty and self-interestedness. How much better to decide thorny and divisive issues by reference to panels of accredited experts, wise men whose training and commitments embodied the breadth and depth of disinterested intellect, rather than various imperfections of the democratic process?

Much of the many-faceted Progressive movement in the early twentieth century reflected the same belief. Although the Progressive movement drew heavily on the nation's deep reservoirs of Protestant moral passion, it sought to blend such passions with an essentially technocratic ideal. Disinterested social research generated by scholars trained in the sciences of government and administration and applied by disinterested and uncorrupted public officials—including "city managers" who would be appointed rather than elected, and therefore immune to political pressures—would lead to ever-improving governance. Such a view had obvious applications in the regulation of giant corporations, one of the chief objects of Progressive concern. But it was also applied on state and municipal levels. Nowhere was this ideal more fully realized than in Wisconsin, where the university was consciously envisioned as an embodiment of the social intelligence of the state and whose president in 1904, Charles van Hise, stated that he would "never be content until the beneficent influence of the university [reached] every family in the state." One also sees the same idea reflected in the growing influence of "scientific management" as exemplified by the work of Frederick W. Taylor.[3]

In the wake of World War II, the "liberal consensus" seemed to be a triumphant iteration of the same idea, although in a more self-consciously value-neutral key, drained of any taint of Progressive moralism. It was in a sense a purer realization of the ideal, offering a dispassionate, pragmatic, experimental, flexible, and nonideological approach to governance. It envisioned the American society and economy as a system of countervailing forces that could be kept in balance by intelligent, problem-solving experts. Daniel Bell limned the scene in 1960 with a not-entirely-approving description of the "end of ideology" and "exhaustion of political ideas" at the end of the fifties. A similar view was laid out in a more upbeat way by President John F. Kennedy in his 1962 Yale commencement speech, where he declared: "What is at stake in our economic decisions today is not some grand warfare of rival ideologies which will sweep the country with passion, but the practical management of a modern economy. What we need is not labels and clichés but more basic discussion of the sophisticated and technical questions involved in keeping a great economic machinery moving ahead." Kennedy concluded not with the usual inspirational uplift, but by advising the graduates to take their part "in the solution of the problems that pour upon us, requiring the most sophisticated and technical judgment."[4] He was coolly ushering them into the ranks of the governing experts.

In retrospect, it appears that Kennedy's words marked a kind of high point for the technocratic idea. The authority of experts took a considerable beating in the subsequent half century, precisely because the idea toward which such authority tended—the idea that expert knowledge could be amassed and exercised in an entirely disinterested way, the core of the technocratic-sociocratic dream—was found to be subversive of any meaningful conception of political democracy. This suspicion has endured and has had interesting and unpredictable ramifications. For example, it has a role in the emergence in the midsixties of "public choice" economic theory, which insists that all considerations of public policy include the recognition that government itself is an interest group and thereby flatly rejects the fundamental technocratic claim of disinterestedness. Such a hermeneutic of suspicion has its own drawbacks and its own forms of naïveté. But it has complicated the picture as far as a realistic assessment of the role of experts is concerned. And it has rendered the technocratic dream an extremely problematic one.

We find ourselves, then, at a fitting moment to reflect freshly on the uneasy status of expertise in a democratic society. The uneasiness is unavoidable because expertise and democracy are in fundamental tension with one another. Expertise locates authority in specialized knowledge and professional certification, based on extensive education and exposure to rigorous standards of evidence operating in highly exclusive self-correcting communities of peer review. Democracy, in contrast, is a principle that tends toward the widest possible affirmation of the fundamental competence of every man or woman, simply as a function of the person's status as a human being and a citizen, regardless of education, social class, or material wealth. The two principles can coexist, of course. They may even serve as useful correctives to each other, as in the concept of an equal-opportunity meritocracy, which seeks to honor them both. But neither principle can easily be fenced in, and neither one can be contented with anything short of predominance. Their coexistence, in short, never comes without a measure of chronic mutual distrust.

Reagan and Cultural Change

But there is another approach to these problems, and it is precisely the approach that Ronald Reagan promoted throughout most of his career, an approach that emphasized personal liberty, economic growth, individual enterprise, decentralism, traditional values, personal responsibility, religious faith, and reliance upon the organs of civil society.

In particular, the ascendancy of Reagan represented something enduringly important and distinctive about American life: its remarkable openness to infusions of new energy and creativity from below, that is, from the nonaccredited, noncredentialed, and unheralded nonelite sectors of its society. That these avenues of fresh energy and creativity be kept open is of crucial importance, particularly when so much of the parlous state of American life, and particularly American culture, in the past half century or so has come from the manifold failures of our accredited elites, our best and brightest, who have sought to transform American life beyond recognition and have had considerable success in the undertaking.

This is not, strictly speaking, a populist argument. Elites we shall always have with us, and it is an illusion to imagine that "the people" can ever rule in any unmediated way. But there are better or worse elites, with better or worse lines of communication with those they govern; and there is always a tendency for elites to become inbred and brittle and enervated and therefore unworthy to govern. This is one of the challenges to which they must either respond or succumb. One of the greatest strengths of American social life has been its ability, again and again, to incorporate and assimilate the waves of contributions of new energies and new blood to the elite class. The steady opening up of our elite institutions in recent years to more meritocratic criteria of admission, even if imperfectly achieved and marred by various forms of preferential treatment, would seem to be testimony to that strength.

Yet there is some reason to doubt whether the intellectual meritocracy, the interlocking directorate of elite institutions that has evolved over the past fifty years, is really doing that job effectively anymore, if it ever did. Instead, it seems to be fostering an intellectual monoculture that is ripe and smug and heavy with a sense of entitlement. It is no coincidence that Barack Obama is, of all the presidents in American history, most fully the product of elite academia, from his elite Hawaiian prep school to his Columbia and Harvard degrees and his years on the faculty of the University of Chicago Law School. His smooth baritone voice is the quintessential tone of certified and accredited intelligence, the American equivalent of what in Great Britain would be called Received Pronunciation, that gold-plated Oxonian intonation that used to be the standard of the BBC. It hardly matters what he says with such a voice, and indeed, a reading of his transcripts shows that he is generally not saying very much. He has no other bank of experience than elite academe to draw upon, aside from tactical lessons drawn from the school of Chicago politics.

We have for decades now had a growing problem of fundamental loyalties in our current elite academic culture. It is entirely fitting that there should be some distance between the two and that academia be preserved as an island of free reflection, where even the most basic premises can be questioned freely, within the bounds of rationality and civility. But that is something very different from the pervasive atmosphere of our present academic institutions, which seem to reflexively teach disdain of fundamental American values and have for a generation or more inculcated in their charges a lack of confidence in the American project in the world. Even students who have never read a word of the late Howard Zinn can repeat his slanders verbatim, because they take them in with the air they breathe. Students know that such assertions are always the "safe" response in an academic setting; hence they offer them up automatically, mindlessly.

But in addition, we have a different, if not completely unrelated problem, which is the rise of an identifiable "political class," now including the leadership of powerful public-employee unions, which also enjoy the protections of civil-service laws. The interests of this class are quite distinct from the interests of those they are supposed to serve, and they live parasitically off of the productive economy. The inability of either political party to come to terms with this growing problem—and indeed, the Democratic party's astonishingly flagrant indifference to it—now suggests to a growing number of Americans that "the political class," those who make their living off of the political system, is so insulated from rebuke that even the prospect of electoral defeat will change very little in their behavior. Elite academia has given us a president who presumes to apologize to the world for his country, while a political class entrenched in Washington and Sacramento and Albany has put us on a path to swift and certain bankruptcy.

It should encourage us somewhat, though, to realize that we have been here before. The seventies were vexed and careworn years, when bad ideas were in the saddle of American life and when many of the overblown expectations of the postwar technocratic elite, and particularly those so characteristic of the sixties, were in the process of crashing down, in the form of stagflation, swelling welfare rolls, urban crime, a general loss of national confidence in the wake of Vietnam and Watergate and oil shocks—a whole laundry list of national woes, economic, diplomatic, cultural, spiritual.

But the seventies were also a time when the very ideas that later countered and corrected this collapse of national morale were taking shape. For one thing, it was a time that saw the emergence of sober second thoughts about the inherent limitations of the liberal-progressive project. Such reconsiderations gave rise to, among other things, the chastened liberalism that was then disparagingly labeled "neoconservatism" and, more generally, to a keen awareness of the limits of national social policy, the failures of consolidated national-scale command economies, the hubris entailed in the progressive movement's embrace of a rationally engineered national society governed by accredited experts, and the futility of social policies that consistently failed to take account of the needs and flaws of human nature, failed to acknowledge the wisdom of traditional institutions, failed to provide an adequate locus of community, and failed to set forth an adequate structure of punishments and incentives that addressed human nature as it really exists and thereby could make ordered liberty possible.

These kinds of concerns were precisely what the rise of Ronald Reagan was about. Moreover, Reagan offered a healthy affirmation of the core of American life, an affirmation coming from a man who was uncredentialed in any of the usual senses. Those of us old enough to remember will recall that he paid for this affirmative spirit by being constantly adjudged a hotheaded cretin, not least by the leadership of his own Republican party in the seventies. What a joke he seemed to be: a man of obscure midwestern origins, a graduate of no-name Eureka College, who parlayed his odd jobs as lifeguard and radio announcer into a minor acting career and then into lucrative flackery for General Electric and a stint in California politics. Who was such a man to presume to reform American politics?

Now that Reagan is so widely and generally venerated, it is easy to forget—but important to remember—how savagely and dismissively he was treated from beginning to end. This is especially relevant when one contemplates both the sources of and the reaction to the Tea Party movement, an expression of popular outrage specifically directed at the political class and the experts whom they employ. This is an example of energy emerging from below, of the vitality of the uncredentialed again asserting itself—even if at times such energy may assert itself crudely, in the manner of an unguided missile. And the very name—Tea Party—represents an effort to claim for such energy the mantle of a great and historic American precedent, the American Revolution itself.

The claim is justified, and it is worth contemplating. For the renewal of American life is not going to be administered from the top down, by administrative or legislative fiat. That is not the nation's history, nor is it firmly grounded in our national myths and lore. Instead, our history indicates that much of the energy must come from the bottom up. One can think, for example, of the enduringly vital role of immigration in American life, and specifically of the ways in which America's steady flow of immigrants has always served to renew a sense of the national calling and reaffirm America's promise, precisely because the life-changing experiences of immigrants have given them a more vivid sense of that promise than those of many native-born citizens. Emma Lazarus's famous poem engraved at the base of the Statue of Liberty did not entreat the world to "give us your well-credentialed"; quite the contrary.

LINCOLN AND CULTURAL CHANGE

Or consider the profound symbolic meaning for Americans of the term *frontier*. For much of the world, a frontier is simply a border, and the word accordingly has a somewhat forbidding aspect. You don't go there, not unless you have to. But for Americans a frontier is a place where you *do* go. It is a verge between nature and culture, where the unsettled has not yet been disciplined into the settled and where scope for the most fundamental human striving is still open and widely available. It is the point of creative contact with the energies of nature, a contact thought to be uniquely powerful and renewing. It is a matrix of challenge and response.

Small wonder that the historian Frederick Jackson Turner believed, even if wrongly, that the existence of a frontier "explained" American development. Small wonder that Turner's "thesis" has lived on, despite its many detractors and persuasive refutations by careful historians. It still expresses something profound and living in the national ethos.

It is, I would argue, the same element in the national ethos that informs a considerable part of our veneration of Abraham Lincoln. In fact, as historian Merrill Peterson has shown in his fascinating book *Lincoln in American Memory,* there have been many Lincolns over the years, some of them virtually archetypes—Lincoln as the Savior of the Union, the Great Emancipator, the Man of the People, the Self-Made Man, and so on. But looming large among these archetypal visions of Lincoln is that of Lincoln as a frontiersman, a common man who was born in a log cabin to humble circumstances, a man whose character and outlook were molded not by the advantages of birth or pedigree but by his own immense striving toward self-betterment and his labor to wring a better life out of the hard opportunities presented to him.

Lincoln was not particularly proud of his humble origins, and he did not go into detail about them. His early life, he once said, could be summarized in one sentence: "the short and simple annals of the poor."[5] Hence our knowledge of his early life is scrappy. We know that he moved from Kentucky to Indiana to Illinois and that he was a typical pioneer farm boy, burdened with the tasks of hauling water, chopping wood, plowing, and harvesting. We know that he hated farm work so much that he would seize the opportunity to do almost anything else. We know that he had little educational opportunity yet was a voracious reader, with a great love of words and of oratory.

When the young man Lincoln arrived in New Salem as, by his own description, "a piece of floating driftwood," he was a nobody. But he soon found employment as a clerk, insinuated himself into the life of the community, became popular, was appointed postmaster, ran for and on the second try was elected to the Illinois General Assembly, and borrowed money to buy a suit. He then found himself thinking about a career in the law.

You could say that this was a rather hand-to-mouth pattern of development. Or you could say that Lincoln benefited from the looseness and easygoing disorder of frontier society, with its fluidity and absence of confining rules and regulations, its steady succession of fresh challenges demanding a fresh response. He did not live in a world where all of life hinged on one's parents getting one into the "right" kindergarten. He could come to a town like New Salem and, in a matter of weeks, persuade his neighbors that he was a plausible candidate for office. He did not have to be defined as his father's son. He could begin over again, and again.

Not everything about this was good, and Lincoln especially regretted the absence of educational opportunities in his own life. But one cannot separate the resourcefulness of his character from the fact of his frontier origins. Nor can one separate those humble origins from his iconic and enduring meaning in American life. There was nothing ordinary about Lincoln. But his ascension to the presidency was a clear example of the common man's potential. As Lincoln said in announcing his candidacy for the General Assembly in 1832, he "was born, and [had] ever remained, in the most humble walks of life," without "wealthy or popular relations or friends to recommend" him. But he had been given, by the right set of conditions, unprecedented opportunity to realize his potential.

By the way, this son of a more pioneering America was also the only American president to hold a patent. It stemmed from his time spent on riverboats, transporting farm produce and other cargo down the Mississippi River. Lincoln had seen boats run aground on sandbars or in shoal waters, and the experience gave him the idea of "buoyant air chambers" made of "water-proof fabric," which could be inflated and deflated as needed to help keep a boat afloat.

He obtained a patent for this invention, "Buoying Vessels over Shoals," in 1849. A decade later, on the lecture circuit, he described the first English patent laws as one of the three greatest "inventions and discoveries" in history (along with the written and printed word and the discovery of America), because they added "the fuel of *interest* to the *fire* of genius in the discovery and production of new and useful things."[6]

This is a nice illustration not only of Lincoln's resourceful mind but also of the importance that he placed upon innovation and the realistic view he took of human nature—that innovators would be more likely to innovate if the legal structure allowed them to profit from their innovations.

So the frontier experience of Lincoln's day by its very nature placed less importance upon pedigree. Yes, it was not universal in character. Specifically, it favored those who were white and male. It was not entirely free. But we can say that the frontier tended in the direction of a rough and ready equality of opportunity.

This was for Lincoln a kind of fulfillment of the spirit of the Declaration of Independence, which Lincoln revered and repeatedly recurred to, in its affirmation of the equal worth of all men and their equal entitlement to life, liberty, and the pursuit of happiness. He also declared the equal right of all men to the fruits of their own labors, a declaration grounded not in the will of governments or men, but in the dictates of Nature and Nature's God. Lincoln loathed slavery from his earliest youth—and shared this hatred with his Baptist parents—but his deepest complaint about slavery seemed to be that it was a form of theft, which allowed one class of men to steal from another class the fruit of the latter's labors. The notion of distributive justice was less important to him than the notion of limitless human opportunity—a priority that was much more in keeping with the ethos of the frontier.

The exalted idea of the frontier in American society goes far beyond the sort of flatfooted material explanations that Turner thought he had provided. It is something closer to an organizing myth, with deep roots in the entire history of European civilization. The idea of the frontier in a sense extended back to the very beginnings of European contact and settlement of the Western hemisphere and to the idea of the West itself as a place of renewal, of beginning again, and of America's naturalness *contra* Europe, a naturalness that substituted the virtues of nature for the pedigrees of culture and history.

Hence, one sees a growing concern in nineteenth-century America, as the continent began to be settled and the frontier subdued, about the loss of this connection with nature and the possible effects. One sees it in forms of expression as different as the Hudson River School of romantic landscape painters, the essays of Ralph Waldo Emerson and Henry David Thoreau—and, by the beginning of the twentieth century, Owen Wister's novel *The Virginian* (1902), which, like all the genre fiction revolving around the Old West, seemed to celebrate the manly energy of "frontier justice" and speak to the perils of "overcivilization," a theme also stressed by Wister's friend Theodore Roosevelt, whose own Western sojourn was so central to his experience.

Turner's frontier thesis, put forward in 1893, stated simply: "The existence of an area of free land, its continuous recession, and the advance of American settlement westward, explain American development."[7] Yet Turner ended his analysis with barely disguised anxiety. According to the 1890 census, the frontier was closed, which meant that an era of American history was closing as well. What would come next? Who could know? Might the loss of the actual frontier also mean the loss of something essential to American life? Would we cease to dream of frontiers and cease to seek them?

If that has happened, one would certainly not know it from our public rhetoric in subsequent years. Interestingly, Kennedy's 1960 campaign for the presidency dubbed itself the New Frontier, a direct tip of the hat to Turner's thesis and an effort to reclaim and recover the strength of the idea of frontier, applying it to the exploration of space, among other things. Or one might consider the rhetoric accompanying the incorporation of Alaska into the Union as the forty-ninth state in 1959, the year before Kennedy's election. The enduring appeal of Alaska to those who go there, the symbolic meaning of Alaska in American life, was well captured by one of the state's most enduring names, which one sees even today on every Alaskan license plate: The Last Frontier.

CREDENTIALS, PEDIGREES, AND CULTURAL CHANGE

What these examples suggest is a persistent sense that there is a danger of overorganization in American life, of an overemphasis upon credentialism and specialization, forces that taken in excess can cripple our sense of human possibility, the health of our communities, and our liberty. President Obama wants everyone to go to college, and he sees this, not unjustifiably, as the federal government lending a generous helping hand of opportunity. But perhaps it is less generous than it seems. Perhaps we already have too much schooling in our culture, too much hegemony of the schooled, too much licensing, too much regulation of experience, too little space to move around and find our own way, to experiment and make mistakes, to exercise the power of personal initiative without the supervision of experts, nannies, busybodies, and others who should perhaps spend more time minding their own business.

Perhaps we have become too concerned with pedigree, with the right schools, the right career path, and so on. What does it tell us today, if the greatest politician in our history, our greatest orator, a man whose command of the English language and of the principles of constitutional democracy was without peer, was a largely unschooled and self-educated man without any social advantages? He was a man who came of age with one inestimable advantage: he lived in the loose-jointed environment of antebellum America, an arena remarkably well calibrated to the development of his talents.

Indeed, there was a time well within the memory of many living Americans, when one's advancement in life was not so heavily determined by the credential of where, or even whether, one attended college. To be sure, one didn't easily make the leap from Eastern Illinois State Teachers College to a white-shoe Park Avenue law firm. But other things were very different. Politics, for example. One of the greatest of America's twentieth-century presidents—and one of the most literate and historically informed since the time of the Founders—was Harry S. Truman, who did not have a college education at all. He began working for the Santa Fe Railroad when he graduated from high school.

That less organized America had many faults, and I do not want to romanticize away those faults. But in fact the worst of its faults was its failure to extend to all Americans the opportunities that a Truman enjoyed. That is a fault that only serves to confirm the worthiness of the ideal itself. For all its imperfections, a more loose-jointed America is more open to sheer human possibility than the putatively meritocratic iron cage of standardized tests and glib interpersonal skills that we are now so proud of having constructed and imagine to be less elitist than the world it replaced.

We need to restore and preserve a less regimented, less status-stratified, less school-sorted, more open-ended America. We need an economy and legal structures that are as open as possible to enterprise and innovation. An educational system that is open to all and geared not to the manufacturing of credentials (or artificial and dysfunctional rites of passage) but to the empowering of individuals. A society that concerns itself with the knowledge and skills a person can acquire, not where or how he acquired them.

I mentioned Alaska. Consider for a moment the national reception in the 2008 vice-presidential campaign accorded that state's governor at the time, Sarah Palin—a working-class woman with a scrappy education, many different jobs, no clear career track, and a working-class husband, a woman who was—like so many women of the American West are—both untraditional and profoundly traditional at the same time, a combination that makes no sense in the settled East but makes perfect sense in the context of frontier societies. Reasonable people can differ widely in their estimation of the cogency of Palin's political views or campaign style and whether she was or is adequately prepared for high office. Those are legitimate points of debate. But it was strange and deeply disconcerting to see her mocked and pilloried for the unpedigreed aspects of her own social background, notably the obscurity of the colleges she attended. There was, and is, something profoundly unseemly about it, particularly when it emanates from some of the most powerful and privileged in our land.

This ought to have been infuriating to many Americans. For with her checkered and educationally scrappy background she represented Abraham Lincoln's America and Reagan's America much more than did either her running mate, the navy aristocrat John McCain, a Naval Academy graduate and the son and grandson of admirals, or the two Ivy-credentialed Democratic candidates, or the three presidents before the present one: Bush, Clinton, and Bush, all having Yale or Harvard pedigrees. When David Brooks, writing in November 2008 about the glittering credentials and "superb personnel" of the new Obama administration, joked about the possibility that a foreign enemy might find America especially vulnerable if it were to strike during a Harvard-Yale football game, he was pointing in an approving way toward a development that is not at all healthy.[8]

And of course this presumes that the claims of accredited expertise are to be believed and trusted. But what if that proves not to be the case? What of the situation in which the putative experts turn out not to be experts at all? And for this case we can find Exhibit A close at hand: the entire profession of economics, which failed completely to predict the financial crisis that has engulfed the world since 2008. No social-scientific field has been more confident of its scientific accuracy; none has been filled with a greater sense of self-importance. "Why," demanded an exasperated Queen Elizabeth of a British economist, "did no one see the crisis coming?" A panel of experts assembled by the British Academy offered the following answer to her question: "Everyone seemed to be doing their own job properly on its own merit. And according to standard measures of success, they were often doing it well. The failure was to see how collectively this added up to a series of interconnected imbalances over which no single authority had jurisdiction. . . . [It] was principally a failure of the collective imagination of many bright people."[9] And a failure, one might say, of expertise itself, or at any rate of our methods of certifying it.

To understand in great psychological depth how such a failure could occur, given all those professional safeguards, we can learn a great deal from a remarkable, and admirably honest, confession by the economist Robert Shiller, who had advised the Federal Reserve Bank of New York until 2004 but kept quiet about the dangerous housing bubble he thought he saw developing: "While I warned about the bubbles . . . I did so very gently, and felt vulnerable expressing such quirky views. Deviating too far from consensus leaves one feeling potentially ostracized from the group, with the risk that one may be terminated."[10] In other words, the "communities of the competent" sometimes behave more like communities of the complacent or communities of the conforming. What Shiller describes is a situation that was rendered intellectually and morally dangerous not by the fact of expert consensus itself, but by the illegitimate way the consensus was sustained. By the fear—and as he suggests, a self-interested fear of being fired—that dissenting views could not be safely aired. We see this scenario enacted again and again with regard to important issues of great public moment in which powerful voices and lazy journalists declare that "all the experts are in agreement" and "the debate is over." Nothing is more corrosive of the true spirit of science and truth-seeking than this spirit of bullying dogmatism. The discipline of economics is now paying the price for it. As are the rest of us.

We may see similar prices paid in other fields as well. As Nicholas Wade of the *New York Times* commented astutely on the Shiller case: "If the brightest minds on Wall Street got suckered by group-think into believing house prices would never fall, what other policies founded on consensus wisdom could be waiting to come unraveled? Global warming, you say? You mean it might be harder to model climate change 20 years ahead than house prices 5 years ahead?"[11] Clearly Wade is painting with a broad brush, but what he says is hardly implausible. Indeed, given the problems that the entire field of climate science has been plunged into by the disclosures of what is called "Climategate," the entire edifice of expert knowledge is in danger of a damaging loss of credibility.

What lesson should be derived from this about the role of the credentialed and designated experts in our lives? First of all, we must learn that the tension between expertise and democracy is not merely a tension between forward-looking reason and backward-looking emotion, between rational sobriety and nostalgic romanticism. Instead it is a tension between two different forms of knowledge, each partial but each legitimate, with a dignity deserving of respect and protection. They serve as counterweights to each other. It is vitally important that the contingency and vulnerability of even the most expert knowledge not be forgotten and that we learn not to expect too much from experts—or get inordinately cross with them when we have expected too much and they have failed us. It is not only their fault, but also our own, if we forget that life is full of risks and that there is always a broader context within which a narrow expertise loses its grip and ceases to be authoritative. In a society awash in all manner of expert claims, we need to cultivate a judge's skill in evaluating the claims, to be as expert as we can in the evaluation of experts. And we must accept responsibility for the chips when they fall.

In other words, experts should have a voice in our democracy, and a resounding and respected one, but only that. They should, as the saying goes, be on tap but not on top. They cannot speak *ex cathedra* or expect to be automatically funded, let alone obeyed, merely for the letters after their names, or the sheepskins on their walls, or the professional associations to which they belong. They also have to persuade, to speak a public language, to bring themselves up to the level of the democratic bar and make their case patiently and respectfully, in a way that passes muster with their fellow citizens. An impenetrably technocratic top-down solution to social or economic problems that does not meet that standard and does not seek the informed consent of the governed is unacceptable, because it is finally a betrayal of the very idea of a democratic republic, however "democratic" its avowed ultimate intent.

We cannot and should not deny the power of specialized knowledge in all spheres of inquiry. But we also should not exaggerate that power and allow it to colonize our lives and suppress our sense of possibility. We should not forget that specialized knowledge is always a means, never an end. There are no technocratic experts in the art of living, only flawed individuals finding their own way. And that is as it should be. That is what it means to keep expertise in its rightful place. As Max Weber understood in the end, the bureaucratization of knowledge and the rationalization of the world lead to a barren knowledge that is not really knowledge, because it is a knowledge of everything but the proper ends to which knowledge should be put. It views the world in splinters and fragments and insensibly and surely robs human life of its own spontaneous energy and grace and freedom. And no expertise can tell us how to respond wisely and courageously to unprecedented situations, based on partial information, hunches, intuitions, and tacit knowledge. But that skill, which is the skill of statesmen and salesmen alike, can never be encapsulated, formulated, and regularized. It is, at bottom, a mystery. Better to live in a society that acknowledges and honors the mystery than in one that suppresses it.[12]

One should think once more of Lincoln and of his great speech at the dedication of the cemetery in Gettysburg in November of 1863. As everyone knows, there were two notable speeches that day. The first, the longest and most learned, was given by the supremely well-pedigreed Edward Everett, a former president of Harvard and the first American to receive a German Ph.D. But it was the self-educated frontiersman president's speech whose accents ring down through the ages.

Hence, when we celebrated in 2009 the fiftieth anniversary of Alaskan statehood and the two-hundredth anniversary of Lincoln's birth, we were, in a sense, celebrating the same thing: the enduring frontier spirit in America, which, far from being deplored, ought to be celebrated and nurtured. In doing so, we will be celebrating the ability of this country to give unprecedented scope to the amazing and unpredictable depths of the human person, depths that cannot be produced factory-like by the right schools or the right social arrangements but emerge from the mysterious and often surprising potential in the minds and hearts and spirits of ordinary people when they are given the opportunity to pursue their ambitions. The example of Lincoln the frontiersman and of the state that proudly calls itself "the last frontier" both point toward the same thing. Both exemplify qualities of character and spirit that are at the heart of what this country is at its best, qualities that we should want to foster and preserve in the years ahead. And they are both most emphatically not monuments to the technocratic spirit. Quite the opposite.

NOTES

1. Arnold Toynbee, *A Study of History: Abridgement of Volumes I–VI* (New York: Oxford Univ. Press, 1987), 1:67.

2. See Think Progress website, March 8, 2009, thinkprogress.org/politics/2009/03/08/36641/brooks-freeze-insane/.

3. *Addresses and Proceedings of the National Education Association* 16 (1918): 687.

4. Yale University Commencement Address, June 11, 1962. See www.jfklibrary.org/Research/Ready-Reference.

5. Benjamin P. Thomas, *Abraham Lincoln: A Biography* (New York: Knopf, 1952), 4.

6. "The Inventor President," *New Atlantis* (Winter 2009), at www.thenewatlantis.com/publications/the-inventor-president.

7. Frederick Jackson Turner, "The Significance of the Frontier in American History," in *Frontier and Section: Selected Essays of Frederick Jackson Turner,* ed. Ray Allen Billington (Englewood Cliffs, NJ: Prentice-Hall, 1961), 37.

8. "The Insider's Crusade," *New York Times,* November 21, 2008, www.nytimes.com/2008/11/21/opinion/21brooks.html?ref=davidbrooks.

9. David Turner, "Credit Crunch Failure Explained to Queen," *Financial Times,* July 26, 2009. The letter from the panel is at www.ft.com/intl/cms/s/0/7e44cbce-79fd-11de-b86f-00144feabdc0.html.

10. Alasdair Roberts, *The Logic of Discipline: Global Capitalism and the Architecture of Government* (New York: Oxford Univ. Press, 2010), 41.

11. Nicholas Wade, "Researcher Condemns Conformity among His Peers," *New York Times,* July 23, 2009, at http://tierneylab.blogs.nytimes.com/2009/07/23/researcher-condemns-conformity-among-his-peers/.

12. Max Weber, *The Protestant Ethic and the Spirit of Capitalism,* trans. Talcott Parsons (New York: Scribner's, 1958), 180–83.

CONTRIBUTORS

Hadley Arkes is the Edward N. Ney Professor of American Institutions at Amherst College, where he has taught since 1966. Among his books are *The Philosopher in the City* (1981), *First Things* (1986), *Beyond the Constitution* (1990), and *Natural Rights and the Right to Choose* (2002). His most recent book is *Constitutional Illusions and Anchoring Truths: The Touchstone of the Natural Law* (2010). He has written for the *Wall Street Journal, Commentary,* the *National Review, First Things,* and the *Claremont Review,* and he writes a regular column for the web journal the *Catholic Thing.* Arkes has been a fellow of the Wilson Center of the Smithsonian, the visiting Leavey professor at Georgetown University, a visiting professor of public affairs in the Woodrow Wilson School, and the Vaughan fellow in the Madison Program at Princeton University. His B.A. is from the University of Illinois and his Ph.D. from the University of Chicago.

Paul A. Cantor is the Clifton Waller Barrett Professor of English and Comparative Literature at the University of Virginia. His books include *Shakespeare's Rome: Republic and Empire* (1976), *Creature and Creator: Myth-making and English Romanticism* (1984), *Shakespeare: Hamlet* (1989, 2004), *Gilligan Unbound: Pop Culture in the Age of Globalization* (2001), and *Literature and the Economics of Liberty: Spontaneous Order in Culture* (2009). His writings have appeared in the *Weekly Standard, Reason,* and the *Claremont Review of Books.* He received the Ludwig von Mises Prize for Scholarship in Austrian School Economics and served on the National Council on the Humanities from 1992 to 1999. He holds an A.B. and a Ph.D. from Harvard University.

Allan Carlson is president of the Howard Center for Family, Religion, and Society and Distinguished Visiting Professor of Politics and History at Hillsdale College. His books include *Family Questions: Reflec-*

tions on the American Social Crisis (1988), *The "American Way": Family and Community in the Shaping of the American Identity* (2003), and *Conjugal America: On the Public Purposes of Marriage* (2007). President Ronald Reagan appointed him to the National Commission on Children, where he served from 1988 to 1993. His interview appearances include PBS's *News Hour;* NPR's *Morning Edition, All Things Considered,* and *Talk of the Nation;* Voice of America; ABC, CBS, and NBC News; MSNBC; CBN; CNN; C-SPAN; Australian, Czech, and Polish TV; eight special PBS productions on family issues; and more than five hundred regional radio and television outlets. He holds an A.B. from Augustana College and a Ph.D. from Ohio University.

Charles W. Dunn, Distinguished Professor of Government at Regent University and chair emeritus of the United States J. William Fulbright Foreign Scholarship Board, has served on the faculties of the University of Illinois, Clemson University, and Grove City College. He has also served as special assistant to the minority whip of the U.S. House of Representatives and as chief of staff to a U.S. senator from New York. His recent books include *The Seven Laws of Presidential Leadership* (2007), *The Enduring Reagan* (2009), *The Future of Religion in American Politics* (2009), and *The Presidency in the 21st Century* (2011). His B.S. is from Illinois State University and his Ph.D. from Florida State University.

Jean Bethke Elshtain is the Laura Spelman Rockefeller Professor at the University of Chicago and the Thomas and Dorothy Leavey Chair in the Foundations of American Freedom at Georgetown University. She is a member of the American Academy of Arts and Sciences and has served on the boards of the Institute for Advanced Study, Princeton; and the National Humanities Center. She is the recipient of a Guggenheim Fellowship and of nine honorary degrees. In 2002 Elshtain received the Frank J. Goodnow award, the highest award for distinguished service to the profession given by the American Political Science Association. In 2006 President George W. Bush appointed her to the Council of the National Endowment of the Humanities. She has delivered the Gifford Lectures at the University of Edinburgh, joining a group that includes William James, Hannah Arendt, Karl

Barth, and Reinhold Niebuhr. In 2008 Elshtain received a second presidential appointment to the President's Council on Bioethics. She has published more than five hundred essays and has authored or edited more than twenty books, including *Democracy on Trial* (1995), *Just War against Terror: The Burden of American Power in a Violent World* (2003), *Jane Addams and the Dream of American Democracy* (2002), *Augustine and the Limits of Politics* (1995), *Sovereignty: God, State, Self* (2008), and *The Meaning of Marriage* (2006). She holds an A.B. from Colorado State University and an M.A. and a Ph.D. from Brandeis University.

Charles R. Kesler is the Dengler-Dykema Distinguished Professor of Government at Claremont McKenna College. He was director of the college's Henry Salvatori Center for the Study of Individual Freedom in the Modern World from 1989 to 2008. He serves as the editor of the *Claremont Review of Books* and as a senior fellow of the Claremont Institute for the Study of Statesmanship and Political Philosophy. His edition of the *Federalist Papers*, published as a Signet Classic by Penguin-Putnam, is the best-selling edition in the country. He is coeditor, with the late William F. Buckley Jr., of *Keeping the Tablets: Modern American Conservative Thought* (1988). His articles on contemporary politics have appeared in the *Wall Street Journal,* the *Christian Science Monitor, Policy Review,* the *National Review, Weekly Standard,* and other journals. He received his A.B., A.M., and Ph.D. from Harvard University.

Wilfred M. McClay is the Sun Trust Chair of Excellence in Humanities at the University of Tennessee at Chattanooga. His previous faculty appointments include positions at Tulane University and the University of Dallas, as well as distinguished visiting appointments at Pepperdine University, Georgetown University, and the University of Rome. He has written several books, including *The Masterless: Self and Society in Modern America* (1994), *The Student's Guide to U.S. History* (2000), *Religion Returns to the Public Square: Faith and Public Policy in America* (2003), and *Figures in the Carpet: Finding the Human Person in the American Past* (2007). He is a senior fellow at the Ethics and Public Policy Center, a senior scholar at the Woodrow

Wilson International Center for Scholars, and a senior fellow of the Trinity Forum and has served since 2002 as a member of the National Council on the Humanities, the advisory board for the National Endowment for the Humanities. He obtained a B.A. from St. John's College (Annapolis) and a Ph.D. from Johns Hopkins University.

Ken Myers is Host and Executive Producer of Mars Hill Audio, an organization committed to producing creative audio resources that engage Christians in thought concerning cultural issues. He conducted his first radio interview in college at age nineteen: his guest was Johnny Cash. Myers has contributed to numerous publications, including the *Wilson Quarterly, Discipleship Journal, Christianity Today, First Things,* and *Touchstone.* His book *All God's Children and Blue Suede Shoes* (1989) discusses Christians and popular culture. His former positions include editor and producer at National Public Radio, executive editor for *Eternity,* and editor of *This World* magazine. He also served on the Arts on Radio and Television Panel for the National Endowment for the Arts. He has a B.A. from the University of Maryland and an M.A.R. from Westminster Theological Seminary.

INDEX

abortion, 27, 42, 48–49, 91
Abortion and the Conscience of the Nation (Reagan), 27
academics: as cultural prophets, 60–62; as elites, 140–41
Against the World For the World (Berger), 132
Age of Reagan, The (Hayward), 42–43
Alaska, 147, 152–53
American conservatism: concepts of culture, 17–18; modern conceptions of, 13–14; Daniel Patrick Moynihan on, 13; Reagan's "new consensus," 17; Reagan's opposition to liberal morality, 25, 27; Reagan's political project, 20–25, 28–29; Reagan's source of principles in, 15–16; typical complaint of, 16–17; views of human nature and politics, 18–19
American culture: consequences of divergent moral and religious understandings in, 7–9; culture wars and sexual freedom, 48–49; fundamental values of, 3–6; importance of values to, 1–2; pluralism and, 6. *See also* cultural change; cultural prophecy; popular culture
American exceptionalism, 98
American liberalism: conceptions of morality, 25–27; cultural relativism and, 27–28; entitlement rights and, 22–23; Daniel Patrick Moynihan on, 13; notions of perfectibility and multiculturalism, 30n10; views of culture and politics, 20; views of human nature, 19–20
American Medical Association, 43
American religious values: changing nature of, 2; consequences of opposing views in contemporary culture, 7–9; fundamental, 5–6
American Revolution, 15–16
American values: changing nature of, 2; fundamental, 3–6; importance to culture, 1–2; liberal morality and, 25–26
antipsychotics, 103
Aquinas. *See* Thomas Aquinas
aristocracy: "natural," 6
Aristotle, 36, 67
arms control, 44–45
Art of the Moving Picture, The (Lindsay), 62–73, 76n12
arts: Christianity and, 123
"A Time for Choosing" speech (Reagan), 15–16
Audacity of Hope, The (Obama), 28

Battle Hymn of the Republic, The (film), 66–67, 68–69, 76–77n14

Baude, Annika, 86
Bell, Daniel, 138
Bellah, Robert N., 2
Bellamy, Edward, 57
Benedict XVI, 39–40
Benny, Jack, 47
Birth of a Nation, The (film), 64, 68, 76n11
Björnberg, Ulla, 88
Blackstone, William, 35
Bolt, Robert, 110
Bonhoeffer, Dietrich, 99–100, 106, 110
Boston, 71–72
Bridge on the River Kwai, The (film), 63
Brooks, David, 136, 149
Brooks, Mel, 47
Brown, Scott, 50
Buchanan, Patrick J., 90
Buckley, William F., Jr., 14
Burke, Edmund, 14–15, 43
business: Christianity and, 123

Cabinet of Dr. Caligari, The (film), 65
Cabiria (film), 64
California, 70–73
California Supreme Court, 92
Cannon, Lou, 33
capitalism, 123
Caritas in Veritate (Benedict XVI), 39–40
Carter, Jimmy, 38
Casablanca (film), 75
Ceaser, James, 30n7
challenge-and-response, 135–36
Chambers, Whittaker, 14
Chesterton, G. K., 13
child-care tax credits, 90

"child development" entitlement, 90
children: cultural awareness of, 103–6; use of antipsychotics, 103
Christ and Culture (Niebuhr), 99
Christian cultural criticism: challenges of, 104–7; the "Christian difference," 109–11; churches and, 108–9, 110; H. Richard Niebuhr's cultural categories, 99–101
Christianity: the church and cultural disorder, 121–23; the church and moral authority, 126–30; the church and time, 124–25; the church *versus* the culture, 116–18; dualism and, 125; lost vision of community, 118–21; the need for a countercultural church, 130–32; Robert Wilken on Christian culture, 117
"Christian Sabbath," 124
churches: Christian cultural criticism and, 108–9, 110
Cicero, 18
cinema. *See* films
citizenship: as a fundamental American value, 4–5
civilizations: challenge-and-response, 135–36
Civil Rights Act, 90
climate science, 150–51
Clinton, Hillary, 43
cohabitation, 80
Commonwealth Club Address (Roosevelt), 24
community: Christianity's lost vision of, 118–21; "deferred," 83; as a fundamental American value, 5; moral, 120

conservatism: Edmund Burke on, 14–15. *See also* American conservatism

contraceptives, 91, 92

conversion, 118

Cook, David, 66

"cool consumer worldview," 130

Cott, Nancy, 80, 81

Creation, 124–25

Crisis in the Population Question (Myrdal & Myrdal), 83–84

Crisis of the House Divided (Jaffa), 36

Croly, Herbert, 20

cultural anthropology, 18

cultural change: Lincoln and, 143–47; Obama and, 136–39; overemphasis on credentialism and specialization, 147–53; Reagan and, 139–43

cultural conservatives, 16

cultural criticism: aim of, 102; challenges of, 104–7; the "Christian difference," 109–11; the connected critic, 101–4; love of country and, 97–98; H. Richard Niebuhr's cultural categories, 99–101; politics, culture and the church, 107–9

cultural liberalism: morality and, 25–27

cultural prophecy: academics as cultural prophets, 60–62; Edward Bellamy and, 57; Paul Cantor on the future of American popular culture, 55–56, 73–74, 75; dismal record of, 56–58; Vachel Lindsay and *The Art of the Moving Picture,* 62–73;

reasons for the impossibility of, 58–60

cultural relativism, 18, 27–28

culture: the church and, 116–18; compared to the physical world, 58–60; conservative concept of, 17–18; importance of values to, 1–2; liberalism's concept of, 20; Daniel Patrick Moynihan on, 13; relationship to convictions and conscience, 119–20; time and, 124. *See also* American culture

culture wars, 48–49

Death of Conservatism, The (Tanenhaus), 14

Declaration of Independence: American politics and, 22; fundamental values in, 3, 4, 5–6; Lincoln and, 145–46

"deferred community," 83

democracy: expertise and, 139, 151–52; as a fundamental American value, 4

divorce, 80, 86–87, 92

Dolan, Anthony, 38

Dole, Bob, 43

Douglas, Stephen, 35

Douglass, Frederick, 101

Dragon Painter, The (film), 76n8

Dreams from My Father (Obama), 28

dualism, 125

Dunphy, John, 2

duty: as a fundamental American value, 4–5

economic crises: of 2008–2009, 21, 149–50

economic rights. *See* social and economic rights
economics, 149–50
Edison, Thomas, 70
Edmundson, Mark, 130
education: Christians and, 122; homeschooling, 92; overemphasis on pedigrees and credentials, 147–48
efficacy: as a fundamental American value, 5
Eisenstadt v. Baird, 91
Eliot, T. S., 115, 121
elites, 140–41
Emanuel, Rahm, 136
emerging adults: moral authority and, 126–30
Emerson, Ralph Waldo, 146
Enlightenment, 122
entitlement rights, 22–25
environmentalism, 39–40
Epstein, Richard, 43
Equal Employment Opportunity Commission, 90
equality: as a fundamental American value, 3
Ettal Monastery, 110
Euthyphro (Plato), 46
Everett, Edward, 152
experts/expertise: contemporary overemphasis on, 147–51; democracy and, 139, 151–52; technocracy, 136–38

family: T. S. Eliot on, 121; impact of the industrial age on, 80–81; U.S. Supreme Court rulings affecting, 91–92. *See also* "Natural Family"; postfamily order

family law (Sweden), 88–89
family wage systems, 81, 84, 90
Federalist (Madison), 18–19
feminism: development of a postfamily order in Sweden and, 84–85
Fifth Amendment, 3–4
films: cultural prophecy and, 59, 60–61, 62–73; Japanese, 63–64, 76n8; Vachel Lindsay and *The Art of the Moving Picture,* 62–73
First Amendment, 5, 6
Fourth Amendment, 3–4
Franklyn-Ladd, Christine, 46
frontier spirit, 152–53
frontier thesis, 143–47

George, Cardinal Francis, 97
Gettysburg Address (Lincoln), 152
Goldwater, Barry, 50
"good citizen," 4–5
Gospel, 122
government transfer payments, 90–91
Griffith, D. W., 64, 65, 67
Griswold v. Connecticut, 91
Guys and Dolls (play), 46

Harris, Phil, 47
Hartford Appeal, 132
Harvard University, 2
Hauerwas, Stanley, 132
Haworth Picture Corporation, 76n8
Hayakawa, Sessue, 63, 76n8
Hayward, Steve, 42–43
health care, 43
"heroes," 22
hieroglyphics, 69–70, 77n16

"high culture," 18

"Hillarycare," 43

Hirdman, Yvonne, 85, 87, 88

History of Narrative Film, A
    (Cook), 66

History of the World, Part I (film),
    47

Holmes, Oliver Wendell, 34

home businesses, 92–93

homeschooling, 92

homosexual couples, 89

Hudson River School, 146

humanism, 2

human nature: conservative view
    of, 18–19; liberal view of,
    19–20

Hunter, James Davison, 120

"Idea of a Christian Society, The"
    (Eliot), 115

Ideas Have Consequences
    (Weaver), 119

income tax, 86, 90

intellectual meritocracy, 140

international law, 33–34

Intolerance (film), 65

Jaffa, Harry, 36

Joint Homes Act of 1987
    (Sweden), 88–89

jokes, 45–49

Judith of Bethulia (film), 67

Kagemusha (film), 64

Kennedy, John F., 138, 147

King, Martin Luther, Jr., 101

Kurosawa, Akira, 64

Latter-Day Saints, 92

law: morality and, 34–35; Reagan's

power of moral reasoning and,
    33–34

Lazarus, Emma, 143

Leithart, Peter, 117, 118

"liberal consensus," 137–38

libertarians, 16, 27

liberty: as a fundamental
    American value, 3

Lincoln, Abraham: ability
    to communicate, 40–41;
    American exceptionalism and,
    98; cultural change and, 143–
    47; Gettysburg Address, 152;
    patent held by, 145; powers of
    moral reflection, 35–36

Lincoln in American Memory
    (Peterson), 143–44

Lindsay, Vachel, 62–73, 76n12

literature: Christianity and, 123

Lives of Others, The (film), 21

Looking Backward (Bellamy), 57

Madison, James, 15, 18–19

Magaziner, Ira, 43

Man for All Seasons, A (Bolt), 110

Mapplethorpe, Robert, 105, 123

marital property, 83

Marlowe, Christopher, 65

marriage: development of a
    postfamily order in Sweden,
    81–89; dysfunctional, 79–80;
    modern trends in America, 80;
    trends of a postfamily order in
    America, 89–93; U.S. Supreme
    Court rulings affecting, 91

Marriage Code (Sweden), 82–83

marriage laws (Sweden), 82–83,
    85–86

"marriage tax penalty," 90

Marvin v. Marvin, 92

"maternalism," 84
McCain, John, 149
McLuhan, Marshall, 69, 70
medical care, 43
Meese, Edwin, 27
meritocracy: as a fundamental American value, 6; intellectual, 140
Mill, John Stuart, 34
Mills, Wilbur, 90
Mohler, Albert J., 92
monasticism, 110
moral authority, 126–30
moral community, 120
morality: American liberalism and, 25–27
moral judgments, 44
moral questions: Lincoln's powers of reflection on, 35–36; Reagan's powers of reflection on, 33–34, 35, 36–37, 38–39, 40–42
More, Thomas, 110
Mormons, 92
Moynihan, Daniel Patrick, 13
Myrdal, Alva, 83–84, 85, 87
Myrdal, Gunnar, 83–84

National Endowment for the Arts, 123
National Review, 36–37
"natural aristocracy," 6
"Natural Family," 80–81, 92–93
natural law, 34, 35, 41–42, 128
Nature, 39–40
"neoconservatism," 142
New Deal, 22–25
New Frontier, 147
New Testament, 117, 122, 125
New York Times, 103

Nicaragua, 33–34
Niebuhr, H. Richard, 99
Nietzsche, Friedrich, 25
Nixon, Richard, 26, 90

Obama, Barack: cultural change and, 136–39; cultural relativism and, 27–28; economic crisis of 2008–2009 and, 21; intellectual meritocracy and, 140; universal college education and, 147
opportunity: as a fundamental American value, 4

Palin, Sarah, 148–49
Palme, Olof, 87
Pastrone, Giovanni, 64
patents, 145
patriotism, 29
Patterson, Paige, 92
Peterson, Eugene, 131
Peterson, Merrill, 143–44
Plato, 40, 46, 51n11
pluralism: American culture and, 6
Poetics (Aristotle), 67
"political class," 141
politics: conservative view of, 18–19; liberalism's concept of, 20; Daniel Patrick Moynihan on, 13
polygamous marriages, 89
popular culture: Paul Cantor's predictions for the future of, 55–56, 73–74, 75; forming the cultural canon, 66–69; Vachel Lindsay on California's role in, 70–73. See also cultural prophecy

"positive law," 34
postfamily order: development in Sweden, 81–89; trends in America, 89–93
"postmodernism," 27–28
"Preaching as Though We Had Enemies" (Hauerwas), 132
Progressive movement, 136, 137, 142
property: as a fundamental American value, 3–4; marital, 83

"radical, the," 99–100
radical affirmation, 100–101
Ratzinger, Joseph (Pope Benedict XVI), 39–40, 131
Reagan, Ronald: arms control and the Soviets, 44–45; "A Time for Choosing" speech, 15–16; belief in the American family, 93; Lou Cannon's "Reaganism of the Week," 33; conservative political project of, 20–25, 28–29; cultural change and, 139–43; "new consensus," 17; opposition to liberal morality, 25, 27; patriotism and, 29; philosophy embedded in jokes, 45–49; political successes, 21–22; powers of reflection on moral questions, 33–34, 35, 36–37, 38–39, 40–42; practical wisdom, 43–45; public intellectuals and, 42–43; the recovery of culture and, 49–50; second American Revolution, 16, 28–29; source of conservative principles, 15–16; State of the Union addresses, 16, 22; on subsidies, 38
Reagan Revolution, 28–29
"Red Years" (Sweden), 85–87
"registered partnerships," 89
religion: dualism and, 125; Enlightenment view of, 122; as a fundamental American value, 5–6. *See also* American religious values; Christianity
"revanchism," 14
Rieff, Philip, 119
Roman Empire, 18, 116
Roosevelt, Franklin Delano, 22–23, 24
Roosevelt, Theodore, 146
Rorty, Richard, 27
"rugged individualism," 4
"rule of law," 4
Russell, Bertrand, 46

Sabbath, 124
same-sex couples, 89
samurai films, 64
school prayer, 122
science, 122–23
second American Revolution, 16, 28–29
"secular individualism," 85
Serrano, André, 123
sex discrimination, 90
"sexperts," 105
sexual freedom, 48–49
Shiller, Robert, 150
Shipman, David, 66
Simpsons, The (television show), 55, 56, 75
Skelton, Red, 48
slavery, 146
Smith, Christian, 126–30

social and economic rights, 22–25
social contract, 24
socialism: development of a
	postfamily order in Sweden,
	81–89
solipsists, 46
solitude, 110
Solzhenitsyn, Alexander, 2
Souls in Transition (Smith),
	126–30
Southern Baptist Convention, 92
Soviet Union, 44–45
sports, 123
"statisation," 82, 94n4
Statue of Liberty, 143
Story of Cinema, The (Shipman),
	66
subsidies, 38
Sveriges rikes lag (Swedish law), 82
Sweden: development of a
	postfamily order in, 81–89

Tamburlaine (Marlowe), 65
Tanenhaus, Sam, 14
taxation, 86, 90
Tax Reform bill of 1969, 90
Tea Party movement, 142
technocracy, 136–38
Thomas Aquinas, 35, 36
Thoreau, Henry David, 146
time, 124–25
Time Out New York, 105
To Change the World (Hunter),
	120
Tocqueville, Alexis de, 8, 107
Toynbee, Arnold, 135
"traditional American values," 25
Triumph of the Therapeutic, The
	(Rieff), 119
Truman, Harry S., 148

Turner, Frederick Jackson, 143,
	146–47

U.S. Constitution: conservatives'
	reverence for, 19; fundamental
	values in, 3–4, 5, 6; Barack
	Obama and, 28
U.S. Supreme Court, 91–92

values: importance to culture, 1–2;
	liberal morality and, 25–26;
	moral community and, 120.
	See also American values
"values voter," 25–26
van Hise, Charles, 137
Virginian, The (Wister), 146
virtue, 23–24

Wade, Nicholas, 150
Walzer, Michael, 101
Washington Post, 33
Weaver, Richard, 119
Weber, Max, 25, 152
welfare state: in America, 90–91
Wilken, Robert, 115, 116, 117, 131
Williams, D. H., 116
Wilson, Don, 47
Wisconsin, 137
Wister, Owen, 146
women: employment in Sweden,
	87–88; family wage systems
	and, 81
Worthington, William, 76n8

Youngman, Henny, 45–46
youth culture, 121–22

Zinn, Howard, 141

	DATE DUE		

Concordia College Library
Bronxville, NY 10708